"Lewis and Diane are the ideal couple to be doing relationship work. Their own loving relationship and their ability to communicate effectively with each other serve as a role model to others. They bring their own life experience and extensive study in the field of relationships to their work. They each have a warm, caring personality and a great sense of humor, which result in an excellent teaching style. And they are passionate in their mission of helping couples experience joyful, loving relationships."

–**Janet Attwood,**
Author of the New York Times bestseller, *The Passion Test*

"Just the introduction to Diane and Lewis Denbaum's book, Madly in Love Forever, was enough to make me want to read more. I have known Diane and Lewis personally for over 15 years. The fact that they want to share what they have learned with people is a true gift."

–**Carol Kline,**
Bestselling co-author of *Chicken Soup for the Pet Lover's Soul*
and other books in the series

"Fantastic! Diane and Lewis have written a gem of a book. Millions of people will devour this book and be Madly in Love Forever.

This is not a book of therapy or "clinical" recommendations. These are the hard-earned lessons of two people just like you and me, lessons that helped them learn how to love again— at a level they could previously only imagine and yearn for. This is a wealth of information and heartfelt stories that will show you how to put an end to the loneliness and frustration of "relationship suffering."

Want to love and be loved forever? Read this amazing book so that you can enjoy being in relationships again. And, since this is a true "his and hers" book, make sure your lover has their own copy!"

–**Vic Johnson**
Founder, As A ManThinketh and author of the best-selling
***Day by Day* With James Allen**

"Since more than 50% of couples go through divorce, there is deep need for men and women to find ways to do relationships differently. Lewis and Diane, who have both been through a divorce, have found ways to do their relationship differently and have a vast store of tools to share with other couples. Their dedication and passion for couples to heal and grow together is evident in the way they relate to each other, as well as in their work with couples."

–**Char Tosi, Co-Founder and Presenter of "A Couples Weekend."**

"I was delighted when Lewis and Diane asked me to engineer the audio version of their book, <u>Madly in Love Forever</u>. Being in the process of reuniting with my ex-wife five years after a heart rending divorce, I was very curious what they would have to say and how it would differ from the many other books on relationships I had read. Well, it couldn't have been more timely. Tears of recognition were followed by the strength of resolve and knowledge as their

story unfolded before my ears. I couldn't believe my luck at having to scrutinize their every word several times over, just before leaving on a trip to visit my wife and daughter in hopes of galvanizing the next steps towards recreating our family. Their down to earth, practical wisdom is punctuated regularly with simple but profound action steps that effectively facilitate unconditional love and truly taking responsibility for creating one's life. Their words continue to echo as I walk the path they outlined. Thank you, Lewis and Diane for taking the initiative to realize your own goals and then show us the way."

–Tim Britton,
Renowned musician and owner of Pied Piper Productions

"As soon as I read Madly in Love Forever, I ordered two more copies for my daughters, both single and still just at the beginning of their learning curve about relationships. It's very helpful, whatever one's natural ability in this area of life and however much experience one has. I have been married for 36 years, and I was reminded of many useful practices. Diane and Lewis' book makes many profound and practical points on how to nurture, love and respect your partner for the sake of the full blossoming of love—which is why we get into relationship in the first place!

–Sheila Ross

"My husband Jonas and I had coaching sessions with Diane and Lewis many times. Every time the support and guidance they offered ended in wonderful results for me on the mental and emotional levels. These results gave me a deeper connection with my husband and our marriage grew stronger and sweeter.

Lewis and Diane inspire trust and inspiration through the example of their own marriage and their love of helping others."

–Sandra Magram

"Even after being married for over 27 years and doing lots of relationship "work" together, my wife Sandra and I have benefited greatly from Lewis and Diane's guidance. Our communication is more open, more frequent, and more effective and, as a result, our love for one another flows more freely and fully. It is evident that Lewis and Diane walk their talk and that their teaching is based on their own successful practice. I wholeheartedly recommend them to any couple seeking a more loving, honest, and intimate relationship."

–Jonas Magram, singer/songwriter for Jonas & the Seventh Ray

"Lewis and Diane are the ideal couple to be doing relationship work. Their own loving relationship and their ability to communicate effectively with each other serves as a role model to others. They bring their own life experience and extensive study in the field of relationships to their work. They each have a warm, caring personality and a great sense of humor, which results in an excellent teaching style."

–Jim and Linda Brooks
Certified Shadow Work® facilitators and coaches and couples retreat leaders.

MADLY IN LOVE FOREVER:
A GUIDE TO TRUE AND LASTING LOVE

DIANE AND LEWIS DENBAUM

Transformations, Inc.
Fairfield, IA 52556

Published by
Transformations, Inc
PO Box 189
Fairfield, IA 52556

Cover Design: Joni McPherson

Interior Design: JustYourType.biz

1st printing, 2010

EAN-13: 9781453611289
ISBN: 1453611282

Printed in the United States of America

We dedicate this book to our marriage,
the proving ground for all that we have learned.

ACKNOWLEDGMENTS

We would like to thank Vic Johnson for encouraging us to write this book, coaching us from start to finish and providing us with great advice and direction.

Thanks to Cindy Buck for being the best editor possible. She helped clarify concepts and brought our stories to life. Her excitement kept us moving forward and she is absolutely delightful to work with.
We thank Maharishi Mahesh Yogi, our first spiritual teacher, who taught us how to mediate and who showed us that life can and should be lived to its fullest.

We thank Sai Maa Lakshmi Devi, who taught us how to love ourselves so that we can be in relationship fully with others.

To the many other teachers who we have learned from during our lives, including A Justin Sterling, Jack Canfield, David Deida, Janet Attwood, Rich and Char Tosi, Earl Nightingale, Wayne Dyer, Byron Katie, Gary Chapman, Don Miquel Ruiz, C, Angela DeJulio Warren, and George Wayne.

We have benefited enormously from the Landmark Forum and The New Warrior Training Adventure; we use their wisdom daily.

Finally, we are deeply gratefully for the extraordinary love and support we have received from our family, friends and men's and women's groups throughout our lives.

TABLE OF CONTENTS

Welcome to *Madly in Love Forever*

Our quest has taken us a long way. In fact, the two of us feel like we've been all the way down to Hell...and back! We both hit rock bottom in earlier marriages and experienced the anger, frustration, hurt, guilt, and all-around misery of divorce. During those years, we both made our situations worse by not handling our feelings and relationships very well. How could we? We had no idea what we were doing. We weren't just in Hell; we were LOST in Hell!

Today we're happily married to each other and have successfully blended the two of our five children still living at home. We've never known such contentment with a partner, such stress-free interactions with our teenagers, or such harmony in a home. It isn't a stretch to say that we feel like we've traveled from Hell all the way to Heaven!

We did A LOT of homework to get here, studying the whole field of self-help and relationships in depth. We have read dozens of books, taken lots of seminars and spent countless hours sitting in men's and women's circles. We've attended meditation courses and spiritual retreats and sat in the company of great teachers, authors and coaches, absorbing their wisdom. We've drawn strength and insight from our parents and our different religious faiths—Diane is Catholic and Lewis is Jewish—and we've learned from our interfaith marriage.

Over time, it's been obvious what has worked for us and what hasn't. Seeing this, we've realized that we can save people a lot of time and money by sharing the things that have worked. This is our joy: we've found that one of the first things that happens when you get happy is that you want others to be happy, too.

All humans yearn for good relationships, and research shows that having them is one of the strongest predictors of happiness. But creating a good relationship, and especially a happy marriage, takes work and it takes discipline. If you are willing to learn new skills and practice them, this is the book for you.

We are committed to helping you improve your relationships—especially if you are:

- A divorced person or couple who plans to be or is remarried, possibly with blended families and households.
- A couple who wants to reinvent your relationship and once again experience the joy that brought you together.
- A couple that finds you need approaches to solving relationship problems that bring you closer together instead of driving you apart.
- A single person who wants to be in a great relationship and attract the perfect mate. (And if you are young and looking for "wisdom from the elders," here we are!)

We're thrilled that you're here!

We feel that we are living proof that you CAN learn how to create joyful, fulfilling relationships. We're happy to be a part of your quest for a deeply fulfilling relationship that only gets better over time. In our experience, the journey can be a richly rewarding one, and we're eager to share all the concepts and tools that have worked for us. We welcome you to read on and use the knowledge and the tools that are also offered in our Madly in Love Forever Coaching and in this book to create the rewarding, loving life you deserve.

Blessings to you as you begin the journey to being madly in love forever.

Diane and Lewis

PART I

RETREATING INTO YOUR SHELL

Have you ever seen a turtle respond to danger by retreating into its shell? We've only seen it on the Discovery Channel. But who hasn't thought, wow, what a cool trick….wish I could do that!

Well, as a matter of fact, humans can do that…in our own way. When something as painful as divorce or a major breakup happens in our lives, people usually retreat from the world—emotionally, mentally and physically—for a period of time. Many of us might stay home more, sleep more, watch more TV, curl up with a book, and in general get out to socialize less. When we do go out, we are likely to feel it's hard to connect with others. Sometimes it seems like we're walled off in our own world.

This is natural. When we are wounded, we need to retreat to a safe environment in which to heal and regain our strength. And being less active has its advantages: it gives us the time to put more attention on our own personal growth. How can we prepare ourselves for greater success in our next relationship? How can we open our hearts more, be stronger inside ourselves and more lovable and giving to those around us? Whether we have ended a relationship or are struggling with the one we're in, this is the time to learn and grow personally, whether through reading books, seeing a counselor, enrolling in Madly in Love Forever Coaching or other workshops, turning more toward our faith, or whatever else might work for us.

We think the turtle's behavior is a good analogy for the process we've been through with our relationships. In Chapter 1, let's start with the first event: The turtle is walking along the bank of a pond when suddenly, it's under attack!

1. Disaster Hits Home

We were both married to others in the past, and the endings of those marriages….well, they weren't pretty. We want to start off by telling you our personal stories so you can get to know a bit about us and where we're coming from.

First, Diane tells the story of how her life was turned upside down.

> I was sitting in the bedroom rocking Lucas, my six-week-old baby boy. Ash and Hopi, age seven and five, were tucked into their bunk beds in the next room. I had cleaned up the kitchen and left a pot of soup warming on the stove. My mom was visiting, and I could sense the uneasy vibe coming from her room. My husband had been making a habit of coming home late, and Mom had expressed her concern to me. I didn't blame her because I was feeling it too. Bob didn't seem happy, and I was always wondering, what can I do?
>
> I heard a noise and looked up to see Bob standing in the doorway.
>
> "Diane," he said quietly, "I want to talk to you," He came in and sat down on the bed.
>
> "There's never any right time to say this," he said. Then he laid his hand on his heart. "I am not happy. I've had pain in my chest for two years, and I can't take it anymore."
>
> I froze. I couldn't compute what he was saying. Could this really be happening?
>
> Then he told me that he had fallen in love with someone else.

I suddenly understood what he was saying. As Lucas slept in my arms, I grasped his shoulder and said, "Bob, you can't go anywhere. We have three children. You can't be leaving me."

But he could, and he was. Suddenly I was faced with the fact that after what I perceived to be ten good years of marriage, we had truly grown apart. What a contrast to the happy times when we first met.

Eighteen years earlier, when I had moved to Australia to teach elementary school, I had been swept off my feet by this charismatic, light-hearted Aussie meditation teacher. We fell in love, and three years later were married. Over the next six years, we bought a house on the beach north of Sydney and started our family. After the birth of our second child, we decided to move to Fairfield, Iowa, to be closer to my family.

Our lives were different in Iowa, less carefree, and I began to notice that my relationship with Bob was changing. It seemed as if his Aussie free spirit was cramped by my desire for a conventional family life. He seemed distant and preoccupied, more interested in convertible cars rather than putting together a picnic table, and our disagreements grew more intense. I thought his behavior was due to the many changes in our lives at that time. Bob was starting a new job, we had just purchased a new home and a new car, and our third baby was on the way, all of this could have been the beginning of building our family life in Iowa.

But it wasn't. Our disagreements were much more serious than that. Bob and I had our different perspectives on the responsibility associated with parenting our children and creating a home for all of us. I didn't know how to make it through the inevitable rough times. I was angry, resentful, and shut down. Our arguments were intense. Later I would find out that Bob was beginning a relationship with someone else. He didn't want to be bugged or nagged as he would say. Could tools have saved our marriage? I don't know.

If we possessed the tools that Lewis and I now have, maybe we wouldn't have disconnected in the first place or we could have at least had a more amicable divorce.

As it was, the two-year divorce process was a time of almost constant misunderstanding and suffering. I was devastated for myself and the children. I hated that these precious, innocent lives were being subjected to the trauma of a broken home and warring parents. And, of course, I blamed it all on Bob and his girlfriend. An affair is a devastating betrayal, and for a while I was consumed with rage. In the days after Bob's announcement, the anger would rise up in me like a scary stranger. I would scream, throw pots, and slam cupboards. I hate thinking back on those days. My anger was so intense that Bob actually had a family counseling service come and interview me, hoping that he would be awarded full custody of the kids. Talk about hell. Fortunately, the counselors concluded that my behavior was normal under the circumstances, so we ended up with joint custody. Still I was shaken to the core: I had lost my husband, and my life, as I had known it, was over.

Over the next year, I went for counseling and began to learn how to communicate more effectively and deal with my emotions in a healthier way. I still had to interact with Bob every day, but now I could handle myself with dignity. I learned that I could maintain my self-respect and minimize the damage caused by my strong feelings. I learned to be a more real and happy person as I learned to manage myself and my relationships.

Thank God, I learned to manage myself because one month after signing our divorce decree Bob moved from Iowa to California. Visitation was shared but my hell was living with my three children without his consistent financial support. He decided to blow off the terms of the divorce agreement without creating a new one. I remember him telling me he knew what he was doing. Well in my world his perspective created hell. The minuscule checks did not come close to providing for the basic necessities such as education, clothes, shoes, coats, health care, and visits to the dentist. I worked two, sometimes three jobs to make our lives work. How lucky I was and how grateful I am to the network of friends and to my family who helped me through those rough times.

Now Lewis takes the stage to share the story of his first two marriages:

The long driveway to our new home curved through a beautiful prairie meadow, but I wasn't enjoying the scenery as I drove home that day. Nancy and I had designed the house ourselves, and we had been thrilled the day we moved in. But three months later, all the joy was gone, and the uneasiness of recent times was back.

Nancy had been drifting away from me for months. She had developed a new best girlfriend and was spending more and more of her time with Jane. They often went out to events on weeknights, and even Saturday nights sometimes found me at home alone. We hadn't been able to talk to each other about what was happening, but the time had come.

I parked the car and trudged up the steps and into the house. I found Nancy in her office.

"We need to talk," I said.

Nancy nodded. "I know."

"I feel like you're pulling away from me," I said.

She looked at me sadly. "I feel like we've grown apart," she said. "I find I'm wanting to create a new life for myself."

I didn't know what to say. I felt helpless. I couldn't control this situation. My life was unraveling and there was nothing I could do about it. We didn't even know how to talk about our problems, let alone solve them.

But I wasn't ready for a divorce and neither was Nancy. We had been married for 21 years, and we had two children, Josh, 14, and Nofiya, 9, who mattered to us more than anything else in the world. We couldn't imagine tearing our family apart.

I had already learned that it was deep in my nature to honor my commitments. I had been only sixteen years old when I got into my first serious relationship. Within about two months I realized I was in love with Linda, and, to my way of thinking at the time, when you're in love with someone, you get married. So I hurried through college, taking heavy course loads and graduating in two and a half years. I was eager to finish school and get a good job so we could get married, which we did when I was twenty.

Linda and I remained happily in love once we were married, at least as far as I knew. We worked together at a non-profit organization and did almost everything together. So I was completely unprepared when I discovered, in the second year of marriage, that Linda was romantically involved with a co-worker of ours. I was shocked beyond words. We were still newlyweds!

I was furious with Linda, but I was also totally heartbroken. I became reclusive and stopped going to work. Linda wanted to end the marriage and I agreed; my feeling of commitment was crushed by this betrayal. Since we had no children and there was no property settlement or alimony, we were able to have the marriage annulled. It was just 20 months after our wedding.

I needed to regroup, so I went off to get more training for the work I was doing. Soon after I returned, I began dating a woman I had been friends with for a few years: that was Nancy. Soon, we fell in love and once again I dove into a commitment. We were engaged in six months and married within a year.

Over the ensuing 21 years, our marriage had its highs and lows, like all marriages. Now, sitting in Nancy's office, I realized that she was right: we had grown apart. But what could we do about it? How could we reconnect? It wasn't just our concern for the children and their welfare that made us want to stay together; divorce just went against the grain of our natures.

And so, for the next four years we lived together in a miserable state of limbo. We began to see counselors, read books about relationships, and try to understand ourselves and our relationship better. But we lacked a heart connection at this point and also good communication skills, so it wasn't fruitful. The pendulum kept swinging from "There's hope!" to "No, this is hopeless," until finally, painfully, we came to the conclusion that we should divorce.

Three months after our 25th wedding anniversary we ended our marriage.

As we went through the collapse of our marriages, we were both devastated. We were almost in shock. If you've been there, you know what we're talking about. A marriage is such a fundamental aspect of your life—especially when you have children—that you can feel completely unmoored and lost when it falls apart.

Both of us held out hope that we could grow and learn from our seeming disasters and come out the other side ready to create and enjoy the relationship of our dreams.

That's just what we did—and just what we want to help you do in the chapters to come. Our Madly in Coaching was also created out of our desire to help others achieve their relationship dreams and see the divorce rate decrease.

2. Ah-Ha! We See the Light

As we struggled through the failing of our marriages, we were wise enough to reach out to our families, friends and others for help. We knew we needed greater knowledge and understanding—of ourselves, of others, and of human nature and the world we lived in.

During those explorations a moment came for each of us when we suddenly turned a corner and saw a glimmer of light. Here's how that played out.

Diane describes how she shifted her "way of being" while attending a "Landmark Education" course after her divorce:

> There I was with three kids, flat broke, my husband gone.
>
> "Why is this happening to me?"
>
> I asked myself this over and over for more than a year, feeling excruciating pain, grief and confusion. One day I just cracked. I sobbed in despair to one of my dear friends until my eyes were raw.
>
> "I need help, I can't do this myself. Please, God, help me," I begged. I realized I was at rock bottom.
>
> Later that day, when I heard about a seminar that promised to help attendees "create a life with a new way of being," it spoke to me. When my friend said she wanted to pay for my course fee, I thought, Why not? After all I was at the bottom. I had to find some way to climb out of this hole.
>
> So off I went to Chicago, and, on the first night of the seminar, in a room filled with 250 strangers, I decided to share my story. I stood up and took the microphone and spoke directly to the seminar leader, giving her an overview of what had happened to my marriage.

She let me speak for a while and then she stopped me. She asked me if I wanted to be "coached": did I want to hear what she was seeing in me that was disempowering?

"Okay," I said, trying to be brave.

"I hear your pain, my dear," she replied. "But I am wondering—how long are you going to keep telling your story? How long do you want to be a victim and a martyr? And how long are you going to keep killing yourself with being a pleaser?" She warned me that my "way of being" was setting me up for a life of disempowerment, one in which life was going to happen to me, instead of me creating the life I wanted.

"It's your choice," she stated flatly.

Feeling almost nauseous, I put my finger in my mouth, making the throw-up gesture. To tell you the truth, I was mortified to be doing and saying all this in front of all these people, but at the same time my inner being was screaming, "Bring it on! I'm ready to change! I want to create a better life for myself."

And in that moment, I committed to becoming 100% responsible for my life. That's a tough one to swallow at first. But I discovered that an amazing shift happens when you take full ownership of your life. You start to attract the knowledge, ideas, and support you had been pushing away with your denial and finger-pointing. Once you say, "I created this life—including attracting my ex-husband and making the choices I made," you can then move forward saying, "Okay, what do I want to create for myself now? How can I do that? How can I become the person I want to be, living the life I want to live?"

Did things change when I returned home? Yes! I stopped complaining and blaming Bob and any other outer circumstances to the best of my ability. I stopped feeling sorry for myself. I stopped worrying and whining and got into action. With my energy no longer being sucked up by blame and self-pity, it could pour into creativity. I networked and traded favors; for years, I moonlighted as a house-sitter/baby-sitter, taking my three school-aged children with me.

Most of all, I took responsibility for how I thought and how I communicated, and my family and I began to mend. That moment in front of the seminar crowd turned out to be the beginning of a new life, full of the healthy love and happiness I had always wanted.

Lewis takes a turn. Here is his story of the moment of truth that carried him through his divorce and into single life:

The pivotal moment for me came before I got divorced. When I realized my second marriage was in trouble, I got hung up on the horns of a dilemma. On the one hand, the status quo was unacceptable, even intolerable; the marriage was so empty. I still loved Nancy, but even to me it felt like the marriage was already over. On the other hand, maybe it was possible to get that loving feeling back. And I got extremely sad when I thought about the effects of divorce on my children.

Willing to do anything to improve the situation, I found a counselor and started weekly sessions. I went by myself at first, but over time I began telling Nancy about what I was learning, and she decided to join me for what became marriage counseling. These sessions gave each of us an opportunity to speak out things we had felt for years but never felt safe enough to say. That sounds like a good thing—but actually it was horrible. I realized our marriage was in much deeper trouble than I had suspected. As time passed, I felt an overwhelming sense of frustration and hopelessness. I wanted to save the marriage, but from my perspective, Nancy seemed to have already made her mind up.

After banging my head against the wall for months, I finally "saw the light" one day. It was at my weekly men's group. The eight of us had been through various men's weekend workshops and had a commitment to be totally honest with each other.

That night we started the meeting with a check-in, as usual, going around the circle and each giving an update on what was up for us. I was last to go. I was feeling really helpless and distraught. Here I was, two years into a rocky situation and there was no sign of change. I started talking and heard myself telling the same sad story. Even as I said the words, I was sick to death of saying them…of hearing them…of being stuck.

There was a moment of silence when I was done. Then one of the men, I'll call him Joe, looked me directly in the eyes and said, "Denbaum, we've been hearing this, week in, week out, for two years now. How many more weeks do we have to listen to the same story?

I got defensive. "Men, I wish I could find a way to make this marriage work, but I have no control over Nancy! And I don't want to expose my children to divorce and start over at the age of 47. I feel completely stuck!

Joe said, "If you had to make the decision right now, what would it be?"

I froze. Then, feeling like it was now or never, I said, "I'm gonna stay in my marriage and make it work."

He said, "What do you need to be able to do that?"

I thought for a few seconds. What would it be like to live with this loveless marriage? "I need to have inner strength and develop self-love."

Joe said, "Are you sure staying in the marriage is the path you want to take?"

I thought again and considered the alternative. I thought about the shame of another failed marriage, the loneliness, the effect on my kids, the unpleasant prospect of dating again.

Suddenly it dawned on me. *If I were to leave the marriage, I would also need to develop inner strength and self-love in order to face my new life— the exact same things I would need if I were to stay!* Wow! I thought. I don't have to make a decision about staying or leaving—I have to make the decision to develop inner strength and self love! Then it won't matter which way I go. I'll be able to handle it either way.

In that moment I realized I had been focusing on the wrong problem. I had been trying to decide which way to go, but really it was about changing who I was as a man, regardless of the way I went. Neither direction was acceptable as I was, so I only had one option: I had to change myself. I had to work on myself and develop inner strength and self-love. Then I could handle either direction—and the right choice would probably become clear.

As the ancient sacred Indian scripture, the Bhagavad-Gita says, "You have control over your actions but not the fruits of your actions." I had to be the best man I could be, and then let go.

In the days, months and years after our breakthrough moments, we saw that, if you sincerely want to get off your old ways and habits and become stronger in yourself and happier in your circumstances, you can do it. If we can, anyone can. You just need the right knowledge and some good support— and both are widely available these days. You just have to go find them and welcome them into your life—and then do the hard but rewarding work of making the needed changes.

In the chapters to come we share tips from our Madly in Love Forever Coaching that have worked for us and helped us get to the happy place we're enjoying together today. Thanks for making us a part of your journey!

3. Finding That Sweet Peace Inside

When the turtle pulls his head into his shell, he has a chance to check out what's going on inside his own mind, heart and body. It may be a little lonely, but it's a lot less distracting. We can get so "outer-directed" in our busy lives that we usually don't pay enough attention to our inner life.

This is a valuable opportunity because, when it comes to having more love in our lives, it all starts with us. Knowing who we are and what we want in a relationship is the first step on the path to intimacy. And learning to love and accept ourselves is an essential part of that. Only when we've made a loving connection with ourselves can we extend our love and acceptance to the people we are in relationship with.

Throughout the ages, in all parts of the world, people of all religions and walks of life have gone within to find peace of mind and solace in the face of life's troubles. In the United States, as a society, we tend to be more action oriented, less inward looking, but these are difficult times and more and more we are finding the value in reconnecting with our own inner peace.

Being still "cools you down," so to speak, quieting your emotions and the relentless noise of your thoughts, and allowing a deeper connection with your heart. Call it your "daily regrouping session." In our lives, we have seen firsthand that success in living with another person comes from the strength and serenity gained in time spent being alone and quiet. Success in relationships also comes from taking care of your own body. In our next two chapters we will tell you what we mean by finding inner peace and taking care of your body.

Diane talks about how she went from not having a clue about inner joy and peace to changing her life by making time everyday to be quiet:

Remember I told you I went to Australia to teach elementary school? Come back to that time with me. Australia is a wonderful country, and the transition to living there "should" have been easy; but it wasn't. Yes, Australians speak English and are an exceptionally friendly and fun people. But I was on the other side of the world, and I felt like a foreigner, far from my home and kind of lost. And, as fabulous as the Australian educational system was, I was not prepared for how different it was from the American system I had been trained for.

So it was a tough time in the beginning. Five months after I arrived "down under," I remember waking up one morning in the home I shared with three other school teachers feeling numb and exhausted. I just lay there in bed thinking, *I don't want to get up. I can't get up.*

I felt unimportant, empty and depressed. For two days I stayed in my bed. The same question kept nagging at me: "Why aren't I just happy?" It seemed like I was only happy when I was with family or socializing or volunteering. As I thought about this, I realized something important:

> I love myself and feel happy only when I see others loving me and feeling happy about me. Is there something more? What if I just love me? What if I didn't have to do anything to be lovable?

Wow, this was deep stuff for me! Phew! But it was amazing—just by being aware of this possibility, I felt more in touch with the inner me, and more in love with that being. And with that shift and that heart-opening, I felt energy and renewed interest in engaging with the world. I felt I had something to give again.

Well, it's a good thing because it was time for me to return to the classroom—thirty-six first graders were waiting for me! Thank goodness I felt physically better because they were wild creatures when I got back in there. I don't think they noticed my newfound connection to a quiet and vulnerable space within. But more discoveries were to come.

My first day back I was happy to be invited by my fellow teachers to go hiking with them in the serene Blue Mountains, west of Sydney, the following weekend. As we gathered early that day before the hike, I noticed that I didn't know everyone in the group. Looking around at the new faces, I was absolutely struck by the peaceful and happy expression on one woman's face. "Wow," I thought, "I want to be that happy again."

I was bursting with the desire to speak with this woman, so I walked up to her and introduced myself. Then I said, "Gosh, you look so happy and peaceful. Why is that? What do you do?"

She laughed and said, "I meditate, I do Transcendental Meditation."

Honestly, she could have told me she hung from chandeliers while eating bananas and I would have given it a try. I wanted what she had!

So I learned Transcendental Meditation, and right away I felt an inner calm and happiness that left me speechless and feeling deep gratitude. I thought at the time, *Funny that I had to learn this! It's such a natural part of life. I should have been born knowing how to do this! I want my family and everyone I love to know about this.*

Fast forward to today. Would you believe that one of the first things I found out about Lewis was that he learned Transcendental Meditation when he was 17! Meditation is a tool that we both have continued to use, every day, throughout our adult lives.

Isn't life intense, with its fabulous highs and challenging lows? In the wild ups and downs of life, meditation is our anchor. What's yours? Do you use it? Do you need to find an anchor? If so, we have some suggestions for you in the action steps below.

Action Steps:

1. Learn to meditate. There are many forms of meditation; find organizations and websites that teach meditation. Find out if your place of worship offers a meditation practice.

2. Commit to meditating regularly for one month. Notice how you feel. Do you handle your relationships differently?

3. Make a list of people you know who radiate peace and happiness. Ask them if they practice meditation or something of that nature. Try doing what they do for a week and observe the results.

4. If you've learned to meditate but haven't been doing it, make a commitment to meditate regularly for a week. Observe the results.

5. Buy a journal (any notebook will do) and commit to writing in it for 10 minutes a day. You can start by writing about whatever's on your mind. Notice what thoughts come out on the pages. Any surprises?

6. Spend a morning or afternoon alone, in silence. Activities such as walking by yourself, journaling or sitting and watching nature can put you in touch with your inner self. Write in your journal about the experience of being alone in silence.

7. Try taking a few days' break from diversions like television and radio. Then experiment with bringing them back into your life in smaller doses. Observe the results.

4. Taking Care of Your Body

Isn't it interesting that an organ of our body is the symbol of love? When you see a Valentine festooned with hearts, you think of flowery emotions, but those curvy red shapes are also a reminder that our love life is anchored solidly in our physical body—and we aren't just talking sex here! For example, hormones and neurochemicals such as serotonin and oxytocin have a huge influence on our moods and so play a major role in the success of our relationships, for better or for worse.

The fact is, whether you want to find the perfect mate, rebuild a relationship or get up the gumption to leave a bad situation, you need to be strong and balanced in your body, mind *and* emotions. All three areas have to be healthy because they're so intimately connected. Without a balanced, rested physiology, you just won't have the clear thinking and the emotional stability it takes to be a good partner and create a great relationship.

In Chapter 3 we talked about the value of meditation and stillness for strengthening the mind and spirit. Now it's time for some practical tips to keep the body strong as well.

Getting Enough Rest

Can it be said any better than this? "Early to bed, early to rise, makes a man healthy, wealthy and wise."

These days it seems like people are constantly complaining about being tired, overwhelmed, and depressed. To boot, many people are blaming their partners, saying they're putting too many demands on them and their time. Is all this exhaustion really necessary? Wouldn't it be wonderful to wake up in the morning raring to go and end the day happily snuggled up with your sweetheart? Wouldn't you like to stop saying "I'm too tired; I can't be bothered putting any energy into my relationships?"

Feeling fatigued creates a vicious cycle. As individuals we are too tired to do anything, so we don't, so our lives get stuck in a rut and we remain tired and bored. We need to break this cycle, and the only way to do that is by getting more rest. The good news is that it doesn't mean you have to find more time for sleep. The solution lies in improving the way you sleep.

We were excited to learn about and use a simple technique from Ayurveda, the ancient medical system of India, to maximize the value of our sleep. Ayurveda states that the most powerful hours for rejuvenating the body are between 10:00 p.m. and 2:00 a.m., and therefore, it is better that your night's sleep begins at 10:00 p.m. or earlier. Going to bed by ten is ideal for your physical, mental and emotional health. Hence the Ayurvedic saying, "Every hour of sleep before midnight is worth two hours after midnight."

Dr. J. R. Raju, an Ayurvedic doctor who treats many Westerners at his clinic in New Delhi, suggests people test this concept with a two-week regimen of going to bed even earlier, at 9:15 p.m., and waking at 5:00 or 6:00 a.m. He claims that many long-term emotional and physical problems will diminish during this trial period alone. If you can't fall asleep at 9:15, try setting the alarm clock for 6:00 a.m. and getting up then no matter how late you may have fallen asleep. A few days of this and your bed will look pretty good at 9:15!

Another Ayurvedic tip if you have trouble falling asleep right away is to remain in bed just resting easily with your eyes closed. According to Dr. John Douillard, an Ayurvedic expert in Boulder, Colorado, just by laying in bed you'll get 80% of the value that you would have gotten had you fallen asleep immediately. So, resist that urge to turn on the light and read or get up and pay some bills!

We found that following this one, simple tip of being in bed by 10:00 p.m. most nights maintains our health allowing us to enjoy our relationships. Of course, in the beginning and still to this day it can be a challenge to get to bed on time. What helps us is to take a careful look at how we're spending our time and eliminate the time-wasters that aren't that rewarding. Some television is fine, but not endless hours. Conversations on the phone can also easily go on too long and eat up the evening.

One more perk in getting to bed early together is .... Need we say more!

The key to finding the discipline to change old ways is to ask yourself: how do I want to feel tomorrow? Do I want to be cranky, lethargic and dull? Or do I want to be cheerful and energetic?

Feeling fatigue during the workday is also an issue for many people. We use power naps as a tool to reinvigorate ourselves if we're feeling drowsy during the day. If you work at home or have a private office, stretch out on a sofa or even on the floor with your eyes closed for 10 minutes. Sometimes sleep will come, and if not, we just relax quietly. It is amazing how much better we feel after a 10-minute catnap! If you don't have a suitable work environment for power naps, you might try taking one on your lunch hour or a break, maybe in your car, or see if there's a room you can use in your building.

Move It or Lose It!

If you want to stay healthy, you have to move your body. Getting regular exercise isn't optional; it's an essential part of taking care of (and making the most of) your God-given body.

Not feeling good about your body can create problems in a relationship. Diane describes the challenges she's had in this area:

> I really struggled with my body image earlier in my life. Because I didn't look like the cover girls on the magazines, I thought men might not be attracted to me. This was a worry, so in an effort to look more like the cover girls, I committed to jogging, and later walking, every day, no matter what. I also learned at a young age about balanced eating habits and to this day continue to enjoy food with-

out gaining weight. I began to feel so darn good on the inside that I stopped worrying about the outside. I believed that I was attractive!

To this day I exercise every day. A lot of my socializing is done while walking, and I love using a pedometer to make sure I take 10,000 steps a day. As a result, most of the time I feel like a supermodel inside.

Now here's the key thing: Because I'm confident that I'm attractive, I can believe in, and accept, the love that my husband showers upon me. In my experience these feelings of confidence and worthiness are essential to opening up to true intimacy with your partner.

As we grow older, we start to lose muscle mass. Lewis shares his thoughts on this issue:

I watched my father go from a strong, muscular man to a frail skeleton who needed a walker to go from room to room, due not to illness but just the process of aging. When he was 75 his leg muscles had deteriorated so much they could not support his body. I realized that this could happen to me, and I vowed that it would not. Since my father's death, I have lifted weights twice a week, and more recently three times a week. I also swim laps three times a week. As a result, I have more muscle mass now than at any other point in my life. I feel terrific, and I bring this positive influence to my work and to my relationship with Diane.

Quite honestly, it's sexy to watch your partner staying fit and healthy!

Listen to Your Body, Not the Diet Books

Do you put messages on your refrigerator? Here's one we put right near the door handle:

I listen to my body's messages with love.

You may wonder, how do I listen to my body's messages with love? Should I listen when my body is screaming, "I'm hungry!" or "I want chocolate!"? What if my body is saying, "I want to eat all day? I'm always hungry"?

We've found the trick is to listen not just to that loud, demanding voice, but also to get quiet enough inside to hear the little voice that's saying, "I'm scared" or "I need a hug" or "I'm lonely." What deeper needs and feelings are getting drowned out by the clamor for food? And, if those deeper needs get heard and addressed, do the cravings for food ease up?

In our experience, they do. We've found that when the desire for food isn't standing in for other unmet desires, eating becomes a whole lot simpler. And when our eating gets simpler, our bodies feel lighter, healthier and more vibrant. There's a nice side benefit, too: when we both feel this way, we act like 20-year-olds in our physical relationship!

We've heard it said that, next to breathing, eating is the most natural process in the world. So it seems like it should be easy and enjoyable to follow a healthy diet, right?

Apparently not. Look at all the confusion about what to eat. We are a nation of dieters, drowning in a sea of diet books, which do not seem to be working. Why has nutrition become so complicated? How can you know what information is true for you? How do you know what your body wants?

We believe that the problem underlying all this confusion is the loss of a connection between mind and body. We're too busy thinking about what we *should* eat according to some system, rather than hearing what our body is asking for.

So, here's our antidote to that mistake. Standing at the refrigerator door, we first listen to see if we're really hungry, or just bored, nervous or feeling some other emotional unease. Then, if we've found that real hunger is there, we listen for a feeling or thought as to what would be most satisfying right now. Maybe it's protein, or the sweetness of fruit, or something filling like carbohydrates.

Then, as we eat, we listen for a voice that says, "That's enough."

This system has been keeping both of us within a good weight range. We realize that we're fighting many years of intense food programming. Have you heard these words, too?

> "Finish everything on your plate."
> "It's time to eat now."
> "What do you mean you're not hungry?"
> "But you have to try my apple pie!"
> "Watch out! That will make you fat."

Over the years, we both have had issues with dieting. Diane says:

> As a young woman, I was always on some diet. Before I connected with my "inner super model," I sometimes went for long stretches without eating, thinking this would make me look like the cover girls. Well, I may have kept the weight off, but I wasn't happy or satisfied. I look back and think my extreme dieting caused more stress than benefit. It was like I had an emotional attachment to food and an unhappy relationship with it.
>
> When I learned to meditate, I noticed that I no longer felt the need to eat other than when I was hungry. The experience of meditation connected me to my body and enabled me to know when I was eating because of an emotional reason.
>
> Until I could truly listen to my body's messages, I learned to eat a healthier diet by being a copy cat. I copied the habits of people in my life who I noticed could eat whatever they wanted and not gain weight or feel guilty. What I learned was that I didn't have to deprive myself of any food if I followed the portion control modeled for me by these people.

Lewis has been learning important lessons from his weightlifting trainer, Frank Pinto:

> I'm slowly getting it as I strive to be my ideal weight. The important thing I have learned about losing weight and keeping it off is this: Adopt a weight loss regime that can become a way of life forever, not just for two weeks or 30 days. Frank puts it rationally—if you lose one pound a week, after a year you will have lost 52 pounds, and it will stay off. On the other hand, weight lost quickly comes back quickly. By the way, Frank eats six meals a day, spaced evenly apart, and has about 5% body fat. He has learned to listen to what works for his body.

When we were introduced to the science of Ayurveda, we were relieved. Here was a balanced, sustainable way to eat right. Ayurveda says, "Eat healthy, delicious meals that nourish your body and soul. Eat a wide variety of foods during the day. Use food to fill your empty stomach, not your heart. Eat only when you are hungry. If the meal isn't delicious, it isn't nourishing you. Enjoy your food and your mealtimes."

You're kidding, we thought. We can actually not be stressed out about food? We can enjoy our food, feel satisfied, not gain weight, and nourish our bodies? Yes!

The variety is the wonderful part. We eat cooked food and raw food from all the food groups and enjoy all the yummy herbs and spices. Ayurveda recommends that you include all six tastes in every meal: the sweet, the salty and the sour, and also the bitter, the pungent and the astringent. We found that small amounts of tastes we'd normally avoid adds richness to the overall flavor. And if we eat slowly, with gentle conversation and no distractions such as TV or reading materials, we find we can listen to our bodies' messages and be satisfied with reasonable portions. The most important inner message to listen for is this one: "Stop eating now. I'm satisfied." A wise teacher, Maharishi Mahesh Yogi said, "Always feel a little hungry. A little hunger is a sign of health." More specifically, Ayurveda claims you should eat until you are only three-quarters full.

Oh, by the way, even though Ayurveda comes from India, that doesn't mean you have to eat Indian food. It's the principles that are important: Enjoy food in all its variety and tastes. Be present to eating so you can hear your own body guiding you. Let food become your friend and give you all the energy and vitality you need. Follow these principles and we believe you'll achieve great health and well-being, as we have.

Action Steps:

Rest

1. Write a journal entry about the way you're spending your time on a daily basis, including TV, computer and phone time. What can you give up or cut down on that will give you more time for rest?

2. Go to bed at 10:00 p.m. for two days or a week to begin with. Notice how you feel.

3. Take a power nap each day for one week. Notice how you feel.

4. Meditate regularly, as it gives the body rest.

Exercise

1. If you don't have an exercise program, find one you'll enjoy and stick to it. Use a coach if you need motivation. If you're lifting weights, hire a personal trainer to teach you how to lift weights properly and safely.

2. Buy an inexpensive pedometer and wear it for a few days to see how many steps you take per day. Aim to build up to 10,000 steps.

3. Park your car a block away from your destination so that you get more exercise.

4. Instead of a lunch date with a friend, make a date with a friend for a "walk and talk."

Food and Dieting:

1. If you have serious food issues, we encourage you to join a support group such as Weight Watchers or Overeater's Anonymous, or hire a health coach today.

2. Learn about balanced eating habits and how to listen to your body's messages about what and when to eat. There are lots of good books out there on healthy eating habits.

3. Meditate regularly, as it releases stress and so reduces the tendency to eat to relieve stress.

4. Try eating six smaller meals with high protein and lots of variety rather than three big meals.

5. Seeing Yourself in Others

In the years following our divorces when we were still "in our shells," working to heal our wounds and grow stronger, we didn't entirely retreat from the world. We weren't ready for another relationship yet, but we were eager to learn more about how we could create a better one— maybe even a great one—our next time out.

With this goal in mind, we each attended a number of seminars and workshops on topics such as personal integrity, self-empowerment (not being a victim) and creating ideal relationships. And we both read lots and lots of self-improvement and relationship books.

In getting to know ourselves, we learned the value of spending time with members of our own sex in a more structured setting. During that period, Lewis belonged to a couple of men's groups, and Diane belonged to three different women's groups. (Today we each belong to just one group.) What an invaluable support system! We learned that some issues can be worked out best with the support of people of your own gender. We grew to value those weekly, biweekly or monthly gatherings, sitting in a circle with other men or women.

Most of our groups were formed at the end of seminars we had attended, in order to help us continue to use the knowledge we had gained. The groups served to hold us accountable, so we couldn't just drift back into our old ways. If you'd like to join a group, try attending a seminar. We recommend Landmark Forum, David Deida, New Warrior and Women Within to name a few. Although much more challenging, try forming a group on your own with like-minded friends, possibly using a book or a DVD series if available from the groups we mentioned as a core of knowledge to work with.

In our groups and on our own, we looked at our issues regarding who we are, how we got where we are, what stories we were telling ourselves, and how to change those stories where needed. We blessed our parents and worked to clear up any issues we had with them. It is often said that we have to heal our relationships with our mothers and fathers before we can have a good relationship with our wife or husband. That makes a lot of sense to us, based on our experience, and it's an issue that we've worked on from the beginning.

We took advantage of the many tools for personal growth and healing that are available today. We listened to affirmations from Louise Hays, Doreen Virtue, Dennis Waitley, Earl Nightingale, Vic Johnson and created our own affirmations. We used power cards we created or took from Don Miguel Ruiz as daily reminders of who we wanted to be. We watched and listened to positive messages through CDs, DVDs and MP3s. We grew to understand that what we put our attention on grows stronger in our lives. More and more, we directed our attention towards taking responsibility for our health, creating our own happiness and learning to love ourselves. We came to truly understand that we are 100% responsible for the choices we make, and that we are 100% responsible for our experience in our relationships.

When all was said and done, we realized that the most important lesson we each learned, as we developed our Madly in Love Forever Coaching was this:

> All that we see in the world, including what we see in our partners, parents, children, friends, and co-workers, is a reflection of what is inside us.

That is to say, the world is our mirror. When something triggers a strong response inside us (or "pushes our buttons"), it is because it reminds us of either

1. something we want to change in ourselves, or

2. an unhealed wound from events or circumstances that occurred earlier in our lives.

We call the first category "If you spot it, you've got it." We call the second category "The world is as you are."

Lewis shares with us an experience of looking into the mirror and having an experience of "If you spot it, you've got it":

> At one point in my children's school days, prior to my divorce, I would bring Josh and Nofiya home from school for lunch four days a week, and on the Fridays, I would have lunch out with a friend. One Friday, I had scheduled a lunch date with my friend Bryan for 12:00 at a local restaurant. I arrived promptly at noon and waited for Bryan to show up. As it got later and later, I became impatient and angry. Where is he? Doesn't he realize I've got to get back to work at 1:00? Doesn't he respect my valuable time? Bryan finally showed up at 12:30, apologizing for getting stuck on a business call.
>
> A few days later, I was still trying to figure out why I had gotten so angry at Bryan for showing up late. In looking at the situation, I suddenly realized something. On many of the days I picked my children up from school for lunch, I was late. In fact, my children had dubbed me "Mr. Late Man." Suddenly, it dawned on me that Bryan's showing up late angered me because he was doing something that I myself do, in particular, *something I do not like about myself*. When Bryan showed up late, it was as if I were looking in a mirror and seeing myself arriving late for my children. Without having that problem myself, I would have been irritated with Bryan, sure. But I wouldn't have been as mad as I was. That level of anger came from my unacknowledged anger with myself for making my hungry children stand on a street corner, waiting for me to take them home.

Many of us have heard that it isn't good to be judgmental. However, as a practice, we can use our judgments for self growth if we remember that "If you spot it, you've got it." Lewis "spotted" Bryan's tardiness and judged him, only to realize that he's "got" tardiness too. If we are willing to look carefully at the judgments we have about others, we will see that we have those characteristics too. Once we know we have those characteristic, we can choose to change.

We'll be honest: sometimes it's hard to believe we are seeing ourselves in another. We may say, "Oh, come on, I'm not like that!" But if we get really honest while taking a look at this concept, we are amazed at how powerful that mirror is. Can you find times in your life when you were angry with someone, and see how your anger was actually directed at yourself?

As we said, you can use the mirror in two ways. In the "If you spot it, you've got it" situation, you see, and judge, a quality in another person that reflects a quality you also have. In "The world is as you are," you see an interaction with another person and may notice your inner childhood wounds. Those wounds color how you see that interaction and everything in the world around you.

Diane shares an experience of seeing that "The world is as you are":

> My dad was a New York City policeman for 40 years. He was strong, supportive, funny and hard working, and he wanted nothing but the best for his family. He had high standards for us. He valued education, taught us to be respectful of adults and authority figures and disagreed with any idea that seemed too liberal to him. He had a powerful and authoritative voice that sometimes intimidated me, especially when he said things like "Why didn't you get 100% on that test?" or "That's a ridiculous idea; where'd you get that one?" Sometimes it was just the tone of his voice that made me wonder if I was doing whatever I was doing right.
>
> Then there was his joke about "holidays." One of my chores was to wash his car in exchange for being able to drive it. When he came out to inspect my work, as he always did, he would look over the car very carefully, bending over to look in every cranny and corner, like even the bottom of the car door. Sure enough, eventually he'd find a spot I had missed and when he did he'd call out, "Oops, here's a holiday." I think he thought it was funny to call missing a spot a holiday, but honestly I felt angry, and I would get defensive.

The wound I carry from this part of my relationship with my dad is that I'll often still wonder to this day, "Am I doing it right?" or "Is everything okay?"

Here's an example of that wound effecting Diane as an adult:

In my years of teaching school, this wound would open up occasionally in my interactions with the principal. I had a great relationship with this woman, but nonetheless, if I got a note from her asking me to come see her, I'd tense up inside and think, "What did I do wrong?" I felt this way even though it always turned out that she just wanted to give me some information, or even praise me for something I had done. I still carried that insecurity about whether I was doing a good enough job. Although there was never any reason for me to feel tense, whenever I received a note from the principal, I would unconsciously think that she had found "a holiday." It helped to realize that in that situation I wasn't dealing with the reality in front of me, I was reacting to something from my past. I was seeing criticism coming at me solely because I carried a fear of being criticized inside me.

Realizing that the world is just our mirror, felt like good news and bad news to us. The good news was that this meant we could change what we saw in the mirror by changing ourselves. That is to say, we had control over the situation! As individuals, we did not have to depend on anyone else changing in order to see a better image in the mirror. The bad news was that if we wanted to see a better reflection in the mirror, we *had* to change. Blaming anyone else for what we saw there was no longer acceptable.

More bad news/good news: The bad news is that it can be very scary to look at the parts of ourselves that we want to change. The good news is that when we face those parts and make the necessary changes, our lives are more fulfilling. A person can become truly free to be themselves.

In Part III, we'll talk more about how you can use this concept once you're in a relationship. It will continue to be a powerful tool for personal growth and also for creating peace and harmony in your home.

Action Steps:

1. The next time you experience a strong negative emotion toward another person, such as anger, jealousy, or resentment, see if you can discover the ways in which you are similar to that person. Can you recall circumstances in your life in which you acted like that person? Observe the benefits this discovery can bring.

2. Write about that experience in your journal for five minutes every day for a week. See if you become aware of other present-day actions or reactions that are based on past wounds.

3. Take a self-development workshop that deals with issues you want to address. (If you've never taken one, we are excited for you; you are in for a great experience!)

4. Join a men's or women's group. The easiest way is to take a self-development seminar and join a group at the end.

5. Hire a life coach or use our Madly In Love Forever Coaching to help you address the issues raised in this chapter.

6. Be Kind to Yourself: Forgive

You will not be punished for your anger;
you will be punished by your anger.

—The Buddha

We were stunned when we first heard the above quote. We looked at the anger we were feeling in our lives and realized that it came from thoughts we were holding onto about people who had hurt us. People we hadn't been able to forgive.

Can you see that, until you forgive someone who has hurt you, you're still letting that person hurt you? He or she is not being harmed in the slightest by your anger, but you are. As Ann Landers said, "Hate is like an acid. It destroys the vessel in which it is stored."

Forgiving others is not for them—it's for you! When you forgive, the pain, anger and resentment you've been carrying make way for relief, happiness and acceptance. And when you feel happiness and acceptance, you open yourself to life's abundance.

You know that expression, "You have to be REAL big…"? We believe you have to get "real big" to forgive. And we believe it's never impossible for you to get that big. You may fight this and have doubts and say it's impossible for you to forgive so-and-so after what they did, and, believe us, we understand. But it is in getting big and forgiving those who have hurt you that a sense of freedom and well-being will come to you…and not a minute sooner.

If you're finding it hard to forgive, these words from Jack Canfield, author of *Chicken Soup for the Soul*, might be helpful:

"All people (including you) are always doing the best they can to meet their basic needs with the current awareness, knowledge, skills, and tools they have at the time. If they could have done better, they would have done better. As they develop more awareness of how their behavior affects others, as they learn more effective and less harmful ways to meet their needs, they will behave in less harmful ways."

Diane talks about how she has experienced the freeing power of forgiveness firsthand:

Many years after my divorce I decided to practice this "being big" concept. I was ready. My grieving process had gone on long enough. It was funny—at the same time I decided this, Bob happened to be visiting Iowa and called to ask if he could speak to me. I said okay and he said, "I am sorry for any pain I caused you by being with Patty."

"Pain!" I replied. "Bob, I've been making my way back from Hell." But here it was, my opportunity to forgive.

So I said, "Thank you. The hurt has been unbelievably deep, not just for me, but also for our children. I accept your apology and I am trying to forgive you without condoning your actions."

From the day "disaster hit home" I hadn't understood certain choices Bob had made, particularly around child support and medical payments. I thought they had had an adverse effect on our three children (and I still do today). So you could say, on that day I began the process of forgiving him but not his actions. And that was enough for my healing process to begin

Sometime after that conversation, many years later, Bob and his girlfriend, Patty, were in Iowa at Christmastime. Patty was "the other woman" who had "broken up" our marriage, so I had never wanted to have any contact with her. However, I did appreciate her kindness to my children and I was also feeling some sense of relief in my heart since my talk with Bob, so I decided to have them over for Christmas Eve dinner. I was inspired by Jesus' teaching about forgiveness. As a Catholic I learned that Jesus said we should forgive people 7 times over.

It was quite an evening. Outside, the snow was coming down, and inside, at the table were six of us: me, Bob, our three children and Patty. Is this really happening, I kept thinking. Am I nuts? With tears in my eyes, feeling all kinds of emotions, I held up one of the pretty wine glasses my children had given me the year before and made a toast.

"To family, no matter how it looks, and to the power of forgiveness."

The expression on the faces of my three children is something I'll never forget. They looked amazed and happy as they took in this message. To see their parents civil again, actually conversing and smiling, brought them an ease that was worth the stretch it had taken me to "get big." And there was no dishonesty. The children were clear that I was forgiving Bob and Patty; I was not forgiving their behavior.

We ate a few more meals together over the years, but that was the big one. There was a level of healing for everyone around that holiday table that made the effort well worth it. And I was the biggest winner that night; I let go of a lot of the bitterness and resentment I had been carrying for years. To this day, I look back and I'm glad I made that choice.

That's just what being able to forgive is—a choice. However "wrong" someone else may be, it's your choice whether to stay stuck and angry, hanging onto being right and having control, or to forgive and allow the heart to open and feel compassion instead of resentment.

Now, we know that time is needed to process a hurt. But how much time? Have you been carrying a grudge for a long time? Are you tired of doing that? Is holding the grudge affecting your health and well-being? Then maybe you are here, now, reading this because you are ready to forgive a person. You won't be sorry if you take that step.

Don't feel that you have to invite the person to your home to forgive them. You don't ever have to see them again if you don't want to. You can do it by letter if you choose, or on the phone. If you want to forgive someone who is no longer living, perhaps your parents, the act of writing the letter may be enough to free your heart.

Again, you are forgiving the person, not the action. You do this for you so you can move through life with an open and healed heart.

Lewis shares his story about the powerful effect of writing a forgiveness letter to his first wife:

> I had heard about forgiveness letters but had never written one before. It was a Sunday morning during the summer. I decided to drive to a lake about 30 minutes away. I took a paper and a pen with me as I wanted to experiment with a forgiveness letter. Upon arriving at the lake, I found a quiet place to sit and think. I asked myself, where do I stand with respect to my first wife, Linda?
>
> As you may remember from Chapter 1, we were high school sweethearts and got married when I finished college. Our marriage ended after 20 months when Linda became interested in another man. To say I was angry was an understatement. After our divorce, although we knew of the other's whereabouts, Linda and I had very little contact with each other. Here I was, 25 years later, still angry over how our marriage had ended.
>
> I asked myself, does it serve me to continue to hold onto this anger? I started to think about all the good times Linda and I had shared.

We had had a lot of fun dating and hanging out with mutual friends from our senior year in high school through college. Then I suddenly realized that my anger was preventing me from enjoying the memory of all those happy times. What a loss! I didn't want to lose those happy memories. I was ready to trade in my anger for them. And with that decision, I was able to forgive.

I proceeded to write Linda a letter forgiving her for the way our marriage had ended and telling her I could now enjoy the happy memories. I got Linda's address from a friend and mailed the letter. I didn't expect to receive a reply, and it didn't matter as the act of writing the letter was completion for me. To my surprise, I did receive a warm and thankful letter from Linda, expressing her appreciation for my forgiveness. Our letters to each other healed a quarter-century-old wound. I only wish I had done it sooner.

You can also write a forgiveness letter to yourself. Maybe you made some mistakes in the past that you've never stopped beating yourself up over. Does that serve any purpose? Not so much! It's time to say, yes, that was wrong, but I'm very sorry about it and it's in the past. I'm a different person today. Remorse is worthwhile, but anger toward yourself is as self-destructive as anger towards others. And it doesn't make amends for past mistakes—it's another mistake!

Ready to forgive someone or yourself?

Action Steps:

1. Schedule some quiet time. Sit and think of a situation that is not fully resolved in your mind and heart. What pain and hurt has it caused? How would your life be different if you forgave the person involved in the situation?

2. Write a letter to someone either forgiving the person or asking for his or her forgiveness. Then decide whether you will mail it, email it, call the person or hand-deliver the message. Wait to write until you can be completely sincere. Do not be attached to an outcome.

3. Schedule some quiet time. Ask yourself, "What have I done that I regret?" Write a letter to yourself forgiving yourself for your shortcomings or inappropriate behavior. This is NOT a trivial exercise.

7. Growing Through Gratitude

The German philosopher Meister Eckhart once said, "If the only prayer you ever say in your whole life is thank you that would suffice." And, not only did Albert Einstein figure out that $E=MC^2$, he also believed that, "there are only two ways to live your life. One is as though nothing is a miracle. The other is as though everything is a miracle."

Inspiring quotes, don't you think? In our experience, miracles can occur in your life if you cultivate just one new habit: remembering to feel and express gratitude.

Lewis tells the story of how he learned about the miraculous power of gratitude:

> During the three-year period in which I was deciding whether or not to get divorced, I had many days during which I was depressed. Over time I discovered that going for a brisk walk sometimes helped lift my spirits. One day, on one of these walks, instead of focusing on the problems plaguing my life, I spontaneously started thinking about the things I was grateful for. After a few minutes of doing this, I noticed that I felt better—much better than I would have if only random thoughts had been going through my head.
>
> I was curious as to whether the grateful thoughts had really helped me feel better, so on my walk the next day, I set off with the intention of being grateful for as many things as I could think of. I walked for 30 minutes, stating aloud all the things for which I was grateful. (I was out in the country so, fortunately, only the cows could hear me.) After a few minutes, I thought I had run out of things to be grateful for, but I was determined to be grateful for the entire walk. So I kept going, and in the process, I got in touch with all the blessings in my life that I usually took for granted. Here are some examples:
>
>> I am grateful that my arms and legs are working properly.
>> I am grateful that I can breathe well and don't have allergies.

I am grateful that I live in a town that is at peace.

I am grateful that I have plenty of water to drink.

Maybe it wasn't the most scientific experiment, but I'm convinced that my attitude of gratitude was effective in alleviating my depression. I dubbed these walks my "gratitude walks." They worked so well, I still take them, and they're one of the main things I'm grateful for today.

Lewis was lucky. Did you notice that, at first, the grateful thoughts happened spontaneously? On future walks he stated his intention to be grateful so he could see what happened. He noticed he felt less depressed, and all because he had expressed gratitude for what he already had. Lewis found that when you move into a place of gratitude, you realize that nothing that you really need is missing, and so you become lighter at heart.

Diane shares her experience of growing in gratitude:

As I described at the beginning of this book, I had hard times, particularly financially, after my divorce. Fortunately, I had my family, friends and community helping me. People were so generous in countless ways, large and small, whether giving me house-sitting jobs or passing on clothes and other items they couldn't use, or surprising me with nice gifts at special times.

I was very moved by their loving support and was always looking for ways to say thank you. I would write thank-you cards, bake cookies, trade favors and help wherever I could to show my gratitude.

One day I mentioned to a friend how lucky I was to have so much support from family and friends. She told me that people liked helping me because, first, they could see that I was doing as much as I could for myself without complaining, and, second, they appreciated that I found little ways to say thank you. They felt appreciated by me, so it was their joy to help me. I realized then and there that expressing gratitude was a positive and powerful thing to do.

When the two of us first met, we talked about what we had learned about gratitude from our own experiences. We agreed that we did not want to get into a rut, take each other for granted or complain and blame each other. We felt that if we expressed gratitude to each other it would increase the chances of both of us wanting to do more for each other and give more love to each other. After all, who wants to give to a whiner?!

So as a new practice, we began to express gratitude to each other. And we do it in a particular way. Do you remember the concept of relationships being a mirror from Chapter 5? When we feel uncomfortable with each other, we do our very best to remember the mirror concept and express gratitude for the opportunity the other is giving us. So, if you were a fly on the wall, you would hear something like this:

> "Thank you, Diane, for showing me the part of myself that needs to be more accountable for coming home when I say I will."

> "Thank you, Lewis, for showing me that I still need to be more comfortable speaking my truth."

We admit that this new way of expressing gratitude takes practice, and opportunities to practice in our Madly in Love Forever Coaching are available. So we ask once again—are you ready for this?—it's another great opportunity to be responsible for what you are up to with your loved one.

Here's what else we have learned and experienced about gratitude:

> Gratitude makes us feel better and more youthful and vibrant.
>
> It promotes health as it releases positive endorphins throughout the body.
>
> It releases us from stress, worry, anger, resentment and greed.
>
> It opens our hearts to love.
>
> It makes us generous and kind.
>
> It connects us to our soul.

Can you now see why gratitude is one of the easiest ways to become happier? Can you see how being happy within yourself will serve your relationship? Are you ready to look at our action steps and create a habit of living in gratitude? We promise you'll be grateful you did!

Action steps:

1. When someone compliments you, say, "Thank you." Don't downplay it or negate it. Give a compliment in return.

2. Keep a "Gratitude Rock." Find a special rock or any object that will fit in your pocket or purse. Every time you touch it, mentally give thanks for something, maybe a quality your partner has. It's okay to be repetitive.

3. In your journal, write as many sentences about your partner as you can, using this template: "I am grateful for _____ because he/she is_____." It's okay if you only come up with one. Repeat this process as often as possible.

4. The 180-degree turn-around. Set a clock or cell phone alarm for a random future time. When it goes off, notice if you are in gratitude or if are you complaining, being unappreciative or demanding, or feeling sorry for yourself. If you are complaining, turn it around 180 degrees. For example, if you are at work and you catch yourself feeling stressed because of an upcoming deadline, change the thought to: "I am grateful for this good job in these hard economic times."

5. Try this one. Put on some mellow music. Sit with your eyes closed, put your hand on your heart and think about what you are grateful for. Think of your relationships, your material possessions, your body and mind. Then write your thoughts in your journal.

PART II

POKING YOUR HEAD OUT
AND TRYING AGAIN

So, how's our turtle doing in its shell? It's probably feeling like it would love to stretch its legs by now. When the turtle feels ready to face the world again, it peeks its head out and has a look around. If the coast is clear, the legs come out and it takes its first steps.

Those first few tentative steps remind us of the dates you go on once you've decided to step back into the world of relationships. Dating can feel pretty awkward at first, if not downright terrifying. After being married, having kids and getting divorced, a lot of people shrink from dating in horror. We can't say we always enjoyed the experience, but we sure did learn a lot. In fact, it was a time of transformation for us. We ended up learning more about ourselves than we ever could have on our own.

In Part II, we take a look at some of the skills you need in order to succeed in relationships with others. Dating gives us a chance to practice those skills, as does marriage. We're talking about abilities such as learning to speak wisely, to listen lovingly, to stop trying to control our partner or make them turn into carbon copies of ourselves, and to get over having unrealistic expectations of them.

First, let's start this journey by wandering into that dark, unknown land called Dating....

8. Would You Date You?

Did you ever ask yourself…

Who am I? What do I value? What do I have to offer to someone? Am I happy alone? Am I ready to share myself? Am I ready to give? Why do I want to be in a relationship, anyway?

We have figured out that knowing yourself as much as possible is the key to entering the dating world and coming out the other side in a happy relationship. Defining who we are and what we stand for is essential if we want dating to eventually lead to something more lasting.

One helpful line of inquiry is to look at why one would want to be in a relationship. A lot of times it's because we are lonely, bored, depressed, afraid to be alone or afraid of what people will think if we're alone. If that's our motivation, more time may be needed in the shell, getting stronger within ourselves before we start asking people out to the movies!

Diane shares what she learned from her dating experience:

> You could look at the dating process as a "practice" like the practices we follow for our health or spiritual growth. That's the way I looked at it when I started dating again after my divorce, and that attitude opened me up to a lot of learning and thinking about the above questions. I knew that I wanted to be in a relationship again. I did not want my divorce to be in vain, so I wanted to look at what I had learned from it, and what I could do differently. And I was determined to not just *do* something different, but to *be* something different.
>
> I'll always appreciate the first man I dated. He has a beautiful heart, and he modeled how a gentleman behaves. He reminded me to be open and to receive the respect I deserved. I did not stay with this man, but I remember him and thank him from the bottom of my

heart for his kindness. One important thing we did in our relation-ship was to acknowledge the fact that, despite not knowing if this was forever, we were happy in the present moment because it was a win-win situation. We served each other in practical ways and in the area of self-development.

After that brief relationship I dated casually for quite a while. I found that some dates wanted sex and companionship with no commit-ment. Some wanted to be with me and another woman simultane-ously. One just wanted to bring food over and hang with my family. Then there was the dance of "I am interested in him, but he's not in me," and "He's interested and I am not." You know what I did like about all the men I dated? They were honest with me about where they were, right from the start.

The relationship I had right before I met my husband was the clinch-er. It gave me some real "Ah ha moments." After feeling deeply hurt by this man, I allowed him to break up with me because, I didn't have the courage to do it sooner—even though I knew in my gut the rela-tionship wasn't working. I waited for him to make the decision after his two week vacation. Why? Because I didn't want to face a breakup; I didn't want to be alone and have to go out dating again. Despite all the pain I'd been through with him, it was more comfortable to stay in the relationship and hope he'd get more committed over time. Nauseating, when I think of it now.

When he left that day, I just let go. On that early fall evening in Iowa, I went outside and threw my arms up to the heavens and said to God, "I just do not get this whole relationship thing. I feel like I should be in one, but I'm not going to try one minute longer. I'll prepare happily for a life as a single, healthy, active, family-loving woman. If "You" have something else in mind, let me know."

My dear friend Lynne came by the next day and listened as I told her about my conversation with God.

"Diane, what do you want? What matters to you?" she asked, ever so gently, and I told her. Lo and behold, she sent me an email the next day and, in a list form, she mirrored back to me what I had said I wanted. When I read the list I thought, wow, that's him. I could actually feel what the man would be like, and I thought, "Nothing other than this."

I then proceeded to live my life fully. No more compromising or making excuses for any man. I felt like, bless them all, but I know what I want in a relationship. I became a very happy and independent single woman. I played a game sometimes where I pretended that God was my date. That game always brought out the highest good in me.

This is what worked for me, and I recommend it: Get really happy as a single person, and for fun, using God or whomever, act as if you already have the relationship of your dreams. And just see what happens.

Oh, by the way, the man on the list did manifest. I am now happily married to him.

Lewis talks about the lessons in his dating story:

Because I had rushed into my first two marriages, I wanted to really take my time dating after my divorce from Nancy. As I began to survey the single-woman landscape in my town, I became confused. There were women I felt physically attracted to but nothing else. There were women who seemed fun to be around but who lacked maturity. A close friend suggested I make a list of all the qualities I wanted in a long-term committed relationship. I created the list and ranked the qualities as either "Must have" or "Would be really nice if she had."

Now, armed with my list, surveying the single-woman landscape, I was clear. I could restrict myself to those women who had most of the qualities on my list.

Of course, as you've heard from Diane, she had her list, too. After we were committed to each other, we discovered we each had our own list, and we shared them with each other. We were both happily surprised to find that we saw ourselves in each other's list.

Here are the main lessons I learned from my dating experiences:

1. **Date to Discover Mr. or Ms. Right: Not to Cure Boredom, Loneliness, etc.**

   One of the best decisions I made when I started dating again was that I was not going to use dating or a relationship to cure me of anything, or to make me feel whole. So if I was experiencing the doldrums, I didn't ask anyone out on a date. I either stayed home or hung out with one or more of my male friends. When the fog lifted, I began to ask women out again. That was important to me because I didn't want my state of being to influence my decision to enter into a relationship with a particular woman. I did not want to end up in a co-dependent relationship.

2. **Honesty in Dating**

   The first woman I dated after my divorce was someone I'll call Karen. We had a pleasant break-the-ice dinner together and agreed to go out again. On our second date, Karen asked me about my spiritual pursuits, knowing mine were different from hers. She sensed my hesitation to answer and told me I didn't have to tell her. I knew she felt very strongly about the path she was following and probably wouldn't like my answer, but I also knew the best thing was to be open about it, so I described my spiritual endeavors. Our relationship cooled after that, and she eventually told me she didn't want to date me anymore.

This was a great lesson for me: Speak my truth. What did I have to lose? If she liked what I had to say, we'd discover a common interest. If she was indifferent, she had learned something about me, and if she didn't like it, it was better to find out sooner rather than later. Karen obviously had her list too. When she discovered I wasn't matching her list, she was honest enough to let me know, and that allowed us both to move on before we got too involved.

It is a big mistake to try to please someone by lying or hiding something, so they will like you. It is a lose-lose situation. You will eventually tire of being something you aren't. Furthermore, when your partner discovers the deceit, he or she will be angry and disappointed, and rightly so.

Don't you want your partner to love you for who you really are? If so, you have to show him or her exactly that, no more, no less. And that requires complete honesty!

Here's another dating tip from Lewis and Diane:

We call this one the "Date the Four Seasons" tip. Once you are seeing each other exclusively, date for one full year. By dating through the four seasons, you get to experience before marriage many of the events and situations that you will have to live through each year together.

For example, Lewis is Jewish and Diane is Catholic. Diane is much more socially active than Lewis during her holiday from Thanksgiving until New Year's Day. For Diane it's party time with all the annual gatherings to attend. While these are enjoyable for Lewis, he found there were too many events too close together. So in choosing Lewis, Diane accepted that he might not attend every single event with her. Lewis, in choosing Diane, accepted that she would attend these events with or without him.

In the summer, Diane discovered that Lewis' job required him to work twelve-hour days during the months of May and June. Lewis learned that Diane visits her mom every summer for two to three weeks in July. Lewis vacations with his children in July and camps with his men's group in August. Lewis realized that Diane would not choose to sit through the long High Holiday service conducted in Hebrew in September. In October Lewis learned that he'd be spending that month eating and drinking from pumpkin plates and mugs, and in almost every room he would find witches, spiders and skeletons.

We have a friend whose ex-husband told her she became so irritable due to the heat in the summertime that he actually couldn't be around her in those months. We wonder if they both might have avoided a big mistake if he had dated her during the summer!

Are you getting the picture of the full range of experience that dating throughout the four seasons provides? We hope this tip is helpful, along with making a list of qualities you want in a partner, treating dating as an exercise in getting to knowing yourself, dating from a place of strength, being honest and surrendering to God. And don't forget to enjoy it! Yes, dating has its ups and downs, but, as with any adventure, the rewards can be fantastic.

Action Steps:

1. Make your own Perfect Mate list. Make sure it is written down. Put it in a place where you can see it (but your dates can't!). Update it as you learn more about what you want.

2. Go out on dates! Initiate them and/or accept them. Make every effort to enjoy yourself and, regardless of the outcome, see each date as an opportunity to practice being more of you.

3. In your journal, write down questions you'd like to ask a potential partner and, when appropriate, ask those questions (not all on the first date!). For example: What kind of relationship you want? What do you value? What are your goals and aspirations? What are your priorities?

4. Date for the four seasons before saying "Will you..." or "I do."

5. Maybe you don't want a relationship. One way to find out is by visiting www.thepassiontest.com/Offer/PTIdealRel/index.cfm.

9. Using Words Wisely

As humans, we communicate in many ways: through our eyes, our body language, and our actions, to name a few. But most powerful of all may be our words. Our actions speak louder, true, but one can do great damage and great good with the language one uses. A little word can kill a relationship— or save it. So it's very important to choose your words carefully.

On the up side, Mother Teresa put it this way: "Kind words can be short and easy to speak, but their echoes are truly endless." On the down side, we all know the lasting damage and pain that harsh words can inflict. "Words *almost* have the power of God," says Jim Rohn. We agree; we've found we have both the power to create and the power to destroy with our words alone.

We believe in using what we call "responsible language." We've given a lot of thought to the following comment by Jack Canfield, which sums up this concept:

> "For most of us, our words are spoken without consciousness. We rarely stop to think about what we are saying. Our thoughts, opinions, judgments, and beliefs roll off our tongues without a care for the damage or the benefits they can produce. It is suggested that you use the power of your words to spread truth and love."

Using responsible language means choosing words that, first, do no harm and, second, convey the truth. As many communication experts remind us, people need to follow these and other guidelines, including: Speak with integrity and say only what you mean. Do not use your words to gossip, which can involve destroying or damaging the reputations of others. Do not vent your anger and other negative emotions on others. Find a way to be truthful while still coming from a place of love.

Of course, sometimes it's hard to be both truthful and loving, but we don't think it's ever impossible. It's an art that can be cultivated with practice. As a teacher of ours, Maharishi Mahesh Yogi, once put it, it's best to "speak the sweet truth." That is, find the way to convey the truth without hurting the other person's feelings.

We don't do this just to be nice to others; it's also for our own well-being. The words we use have an impact on how we feel about ourselves. For example, individuals lose self-respect when they are harsh, whereas individuals grow in self-esteem when their words are kind. And hurtful words are actually self-inflicted wounds. It's been said that when you shoot the arrow of anger, it pierces your own heart first.

Using responsible language is a way to empower yourself and simultaneously get your message across to the listener. We've learned that, when one speaks responsibly, one can be heard, one's needs can be met, and one can meet their partner's needs while maintaining one's sense of self, our peace and our sanity.

We believe that if you are ready to take some steps to improve your communication, the three tools we use and describe below from our Madly In Love Forever Coaching will help you as they have helped us—especially when something of a sensitive nature needs to be communicated.

Using I-Statements

When you use I-statements, you are automatically using responsible language. An I-statement is a sentence that has "I" as the subject and conveys what you feel, why you feel it, and what you want or what you did.

Here's an example:

Non-I-statement: "You're late. You said 1:30 p.m."

I-statement: "I was frustrated and worried. I thought we said 1:30 p.m."

Lewis says:

In the above I-statement, even though I am admitting that I am frustrated, I feel empowered because, first of all, I am being honest and upfront, and second, I am taking responsibility for my feelings.

When I hear someone using I-statements, I feel like I can trust him or her. This is a person who does not lash out with blame and accusations. Blaming makes people defensive and angry; it's almost always counter-productive.

If you have a habit of blaming, as most of us do, you might find that I-statements are a powerful technique to break that habit. Here's another example of how they work. Let's say your partner was supposed to pay the water bill and didn't. Compare the following statements and see which you think would be more effective:

1. "You were supposed to pay the water bill, and you didn't. As a result, you cost us more money because there is a late charge."
2. "I felt angry when I saw the late charge, because I heard you promise you would pay the water bill on time."

If you deliver sentence #1, it is likely that your partner will get defensive and make excuses. And then you might get irritated and go on the offensive. This conversation could very well escalate into an argument.

While there is no guarantee that your partner won't come back with a defensive reply upon hearing sentence #2, he or she is more likely to acknowledge your feelings and own up to not doing what was promised. It sets the stage for a civil conversation.

Here is an example of another type of I-statement:

Non-I-statement: "The garbage didn't get taken out." (Spoken by the person responsible for taking out the garbage)
I-statement: "I didn't take the garbage out."

In the non-I-statement, the speaker uses passive voice to deflect attention away from his or her failure to take the garbage out. In the I-statement, he or she takes responsibility for the failure. The I-statement is clean and honest as opposed to the wimpy non-I-statement. Which statement do you think facilitates better communication?

Here is an example of another type of I-statement:

> Non-I-statement: "Would you like to eat dinner now?"

> I-statement: "I'm hungry and want to eat dinner early. Would you care to join me?"

We attribute the non-I-statement above to "pleaser" energy, that is, the speaker doesn't want to rock the boat; he is feeling out the situation. The I-statement, however, gets to the truth—the speaker is hungry and wants to eat. If you deliver statements like the non-I-statement instead of the I-statement, over time you will feel disempowered and start to resent your partner. The solution: State what you want using simple I-statements.

Reacting vs. Responding

You have a choice to make whenever a communication is coming your way. You can react or you can respond. Here's the difference:

- When you react, you make a snap decision and give a quick, sharp retort, while feeling intense emotion. Little or no thought is involved; you're driven almost entirely by emotion.

- When you respond, you take a moment or two to pause, breathe, and think before you speak. Responding gives you a chance to consider before saying something ill-advised or damaging. It gives you a chance to make sure you aren't just acting from being tired or hungry, or in a stressful situation. You might ask for some time before giving your response.

We're not saying that you can't confront your spouse if you're tired, hungry, or stressed, because then we'd live in a silent world! But, it's a good idea to recognize situations that tend to escalate into arguments, and stop and think before you launch the first rocket.

Words you may hear when someone is responding are:

"Let me think about that."

"I am so angry; give me a few minutes so I don't hurt you with my words."

"I hear you and I do want to talk, just give me a few minutes to get 'present.'"

The way we talk on the telephone provides a great example of reacting versus responding. In our experience, sometimes we get really aggravated with the person on the other end of the phone. It could be a partner, a child, a parent, or a call we don't want to be getting. In reaction mode we've been known to have slammed down the telephone if things got bad enough. There would be some instant gratification, but in reality the aggravation would still be there, plus we'd now feel badly about mistreating another human being.

The simple awareness that we could choose to respond instead of react changed this dynamic for us. Now if we are aggravated with someone on the phone, we can use comments like the ones above, or if the situation is more intense, we can take a breath and say, "I am going to hang up the phone now. I'll call you back in an hour." Then, we hang up the phone, and we notice that even though we may still have to deal with a situation, we feel better about ourselves. We weren't rude and we felt in control of our communication and emotions.

Responding is a way of giving yourself permission to create boundaries and proceed in a timeframe that gives you a chance to act in everyone's best interest, instead of irrationally and destructively.

Lewis remembers using the following sentence with his children to avoid going into reaction mode: "If you demand an answer now, the answer is 'no.' If you will give me time to think about it, the answer right now is 'maybe.'"

Intention vs. Impact

When we speak to another person, there's our "intention," that is, what we intend to communicate to them, and the "impact," what they think we mean. In the ideal world, the intention and the impact are the same. For example, Diane might say to Lewis "Oh, you've been putting in a lot of hours at work lately," with the intention of paying him a compliment for being such a good provider for the family. Lewis hears that, takes it as a compliment and says, "Yes, I'm glad to have the opportunity." He feels appreciated, Diane feels acknowledged and everything is "hunky dory."

There are times, however, when the impact on the listener is not what the speaker intended. Lewis could possibly hear Diane's comment and think she's complaining that he's neglecting her or the family. Feeling unappreciated, Lewis might withdraw from Diane or strike back. In either case, Lewis' reaction is based on a misunderstanding since that was not Diane's intention.

The way to prevent such misunderstandings is to ask for confirmation before giving a negative response. In the above situation where Lewis is feeling unappreciated, he can ask for confirmation as follows: "Diane, when you said that, I felt unappreciated. What did you intend?" This gives Diane an opportunity to clarify that her intention had been to praise Lewis' hard-working nature.
Sometimes, the speaker can sense from the listener's body language or facial expression that their message wasn't received the way they intended. In that

case, the speaker can ask what the impact was on the listener. For example, if Diane notices a pained look on Lewis' face when he hears her comment, she can check in and say, "Lewis, when I said that, my intention was to appreciate you for all your hard work. Is that how you took it?"

Regardless of who asks for clarification, we've found that such misunderstandings can be cleared up easily if both partners are attentive to the other's reaction and speak up right away to make their intentions known. It's simple and effective.

Try out these three techniques today and see if you don't feel like you're communicating more effectively and powerfully. That's the value of using responsible language.

Keeping It Real

When you're practicing using these techniques, remember, you can be light about it. Own up to what you're doing, and the fact that you're trying to change old bad habits. Practice using them now with family members and friends, so you're ready when you're in a relationship again.

Diane remembers how this worked with her first teenager.

> When my first child, Ash, was 16 a lot of issues were surfacing that we did not agree upon. Gee, really?!
>
> Our pattern was that we'd get mad at each other, and I would yell and he would go quiet. Does it have to be this way? I'd ask myself as I felt guilty, angry and frustrated. Once again my quest to stay centered and not yell had been defeated. Determined to find an answer, I got a great book on parenting teens that focused on how to communicate effectively. Okay, I'll just communicate more effectively, I thought.
>
> So now, in comes Ash, asking for no curfew. Instead of getting mad and saying, "No…because I said so…it's my house," and so on, I'd

take a deep breath and confidently communicate with my new tools. "No curfew; that won't work for me. Let's see if we can agree on a time that works for both of us." We'd go along fine and then, before I knew it, he's saying something that pushes my buttons, I'm saying something in the old way, and all of a sudden I'm yelling and crying, and he's ready to walk away.

After going on like that for a while, I tried something new. When we started arguing, I would stop as soon as I felt the heat, turn to my son, put my finger up and say, "Hang on." I'd run in my room, grab the parenting book, read the suggested dialogue about curfews, or whatever the issue was, go back out to Ash, and try again.

You know what? It was hysterical, and suddenly, instead of fighting, Ash and I would be laughing. Deep in my heart, I knew I was modeling a person wanting to change and what it took to do that.

Did he do everything I wanted? No. Would I love if he'd be more open to my advice? Yes. Is he an incredible, independent, good human being? Yes. Is our relationship good? For sure.

Start practicing these techniques now. Some, like Diane's above, are best used in close relationships. Others can be used with employees and employers, best friends and brothers-in-law. Try them out on the repair man who didn't show up, the neighbor who borrowed your chain saw and broke it. Practice, practice, practice, and see if using responsible language doesn't improve your relationships significantly.

And along the way, laugh and be easy on yourself!

Action Steps

1. Discover how you communicate. Stop and notice how you speak to people throughout your day. Write your observations in your journal.

2. Pick one of the communication techniques mentioned in this chapter and practice speaking with that tool for a day. If you notice positive changes, keep using the technique. Try this same procedure with the other tools.

3. Remember a conversation that didn't go well. Think about whether using I-statements could have helped produce a different result. Then practice saying various I-statements you could have used in the conversation. Repeat them 3-5 times, until speaking them feels comfortable.

4. The next time someone says something that doesn't sit well with you, tell the person how it impacted you and then ask what his or her intention was. Look for opportunities to practice this valuable technique.

10. Love is Being a Good Listener

God gave us two ears and one mouth,
so we would listen twice as much as we speak.

—Unknown

For most couples, listening is the hardest part of marriage. Many people say quite candidly that they find it difficult to keep their mouth closed while their partner is speaking. In a magazine interview we read, men and women who had had extramarital affairs reported that their number one reason for pursuing the affair was this:

"She (or he) listened to me. I mattered to her (or him)."

Clearly, it's important that we learn how to really listen to our partners.

Diane shares an experience that showed her the power of listening:

After I got divorced and Bob was gone, my life as I knew it was over. Along with meditation and the peace I found in organizing my home, I used long daily walks as therapy for my broken heart. As winter arrived in Iowa, every morning at 10:30 I'd bundle up in my down jacket and snow gear, and set off, carrying Lucas in his Snugli to walk the deserted streets of the neighborhood.

One day, I spotted another human being walking towards me! It was Candace, my walking buddy from years before when we had both lived in another neighborhood. Every day we had walked together to the school where we both taught. We greeted each other with the warmest hug, and tears of joy froze on our faces.

Here we were, years later, neither of us teaching anymore, me with my broken heart and new baby, and Candace still recovering from a life-threatening accident that had occurred months before. She had actually been clinically dead for seven minutes, and when she was revived she had no short-term memory. She could remember everything about her life before the accident but nothing since, including what had happened the day before.

So picture two women, one with a sad story to tell to anyone who would listen, and another with no short-term memory and all the time in the world to listen! We walked together frequently after that day, and it was right out of the movie *Groundhog Day*. I'd go to her house where her husband would have her ready to go, and as we walked she'd ask me how I was and I'd pour my heart out about what I was going through. Every day my story was new to her.

I learned so much from Candace. Most of all, I experienced what it is like to be truly listened to. As Candace listened, she would look at me and nod and say things like "Oh, dear," and "How sad!" Just simple supportive phrases, but they meant so much to me. She did not advise, judge, interject, project, or try to fix anything. What I felt was her unconditional love and her unwavering attention.

What incredible gifts she gave me: the gift of listening to my woes, and also the gift of teaching me how to listen. I learned that it's all about being in your heart and caring about the other person, not trying to analyze the situation or solve their problems, but just being attentive and caring. Everyday, I practiced listening to Candace as she listened to me, and that helped me improve all my relationships.

Now, we aren't saying you need to lose your memory to be a good listener, though it does make it easier in some ways! But Candace was able to model good listening such that Diane could experience how deeply loving and healing it is. We have learned that becoming good listeners ourselves takes practice and commitment.

Experts seem to agree that there are three "listening styles, as follows:

- **Competitive Listening** happens when we are more interested in promoting our own point of view than in understanding or exploring someone else's. We listen for openings where we can put our two cents in, and for flaws or weak points we can correct. As we pretend to pay attention, we are impatiently waiting for an opening, or internally planning our rebuttal, hoping we will "win" the discussion.

- **Passive Listening** is careful and attentive listening. We are genuinely interested in hearing and understanding the other person's point of view. However, we assume that we heard and understood correctly; we stay passive and do not verify that our understanding is correct.

- **Active Listening** is the most useful listening skill. In active listening we are genuinely interested in understanding what the other person is thinking, feeling and wanting, and we actively check out our understanding before we respond with our own new message. We restate or paraphrase our understanding of the message, reflecting it back to the speaker for verification. This verification or feedback process is what distinguishes active listening and makes it effective.

Can you identify your main listening style? If you can see that you sometimes engage in competitive or passive listening…join the crowd! We all make these mistakes sometimes and need to be reminded to practice active listening as much as possible.

It is crucial that you are fully available at the time of the discussion. If your mind is truly somewhere else and you cannot focus, say so, and arrange an alternative time to sit together.

- When you're practicing active listening, rather than acting like a parrot and repeating your partner's words verbatim, which could be annoying, paraphrase and use your own words in verbalizing your understanding of the message.

- Listen for what appears to be relevant. Listen for the facts, the thoughts and the beliefs in what's being said.

- Also listen for what's behind the specifics: the feelings and emotions, the wants or needs, the hopes and expectations. Respond to the feeling or intent behind the words. That's often where the real message lies.

- Stay with the speaker's story, and let them tell it in their own time, rather than jumping ahead and anticipating what he or she might say.

- Try to restrain yourself from immediately answering questions posed by your partner. Sometimes your partner may be using questions as a way to figure things out. He or she may not actually want an answer. So as Dr. Evil says in the Austin Powers movies: "Zip it!"

- If you are confused and don't understand what your partner is saying, kindly let him or her know that.

- Face your partner when he or she is speaking to you, and make eye contact. Don't allow yourself to be distracted. Don't you find it insulting if your partner is looking out the window while you're pouring your heart out?

- Body language is powerful so avoid gestures like crossing your arms or legs, clenching your fists, putting your hands in your pockets, frowning or straining to smile, or in other ways appearing unavailable.

- Practice being empathetic, accepting and respectful of your partner and his or her feelings and beliefs, regardless of your opinion.

- Notice when you are trying to look good, or be right or control your partner, rather than listen. We all have these bad habits and can often minimize them just by becoming aware of them.

This acronym sums up everything we feel about love and listening:

L Listen attentively and stay focused.

O Observe your partner's tone, emotions, and body language.

V Verify what you heard by giving feedback and asking if you understood correctly.

E Empathize with your partner by listening from the heart.

Show Me Your Heart

Here is a listening practice, we adapted from Robert and Judith Gass, and use in our Madly in Love Forever Coaching that we love and use frequently:

- You will need a timer and an object like a rock, a stick or a piece of jewelry.
- Sit facing each other. There are two roles—listener and speaker. The speaker always holds the object.
- The listener says "Show me your heart" and then becomes silent as he or she simply receives what the speaker has to say. The listener does not ask questions or interrupt.
- The speaker will then speak and reveal whatever is in his or her heart. You can speak about the kids, work, your relationship, anything. The listener says nothing.
- Then switch. The speaker always holds the object.
- Do two five- or ten-minute rounds each way.
- Thank your partner in whatever way you would like to. Give each other a hug, a kiss, or…….. especially after the last round.

And finally, it's time for a quiz! Assess your listening skill with this telling exercise that Diane took in her Life Coach training program:

Are You a Good Listener?

Answer each question with Usually, Sometimes or No. Usually is worth 2 points, Sometimes is worth 1 point, and No is worth 0 points.

1. I often paraphrase what I hear to make sure I have heard it correctly.
2. I wait for the speaker to finish before evaluating the meaning of their message.
3. I refrain from finishing the other person's sentences.
4. I listen for feelings as well as subject matter.
5. I listen even when I am not interested.
6. I listen for underlying feelings as well as facts.
7. Normally, I do not fake attention.
8. I don't judge people for their ideas and feelings.
9. I provide feedback, by saying "hmmm," "yes," or "I see."
10. Having the last word is not necessary for me.

    If you scored 20-19 points, you are a perfect listener.
    If you scored 18-16 points, you are a good listener.
    If you scored 12-15 points, you are an average listener.
    If you scored below 11, your listening skills need improvement.

We hope you scored well, but if not, don't be discouraged….just keep practicing!

Action Steps:

1. Take the quiz.

2. Practice the listening exercise we suggested. Do any number of rounds you want.

3. Practice active listening for one week. Observe the results and write down your observations in your journal.

4. Practice paraphrasing when you reply to your partner. Observe the results and write down your observations in your journal.

11. Letting Go of Expectations

Expectations can be the end of serenity. If you go into a situation expecting something specific, most likely one of two things will happen. If things work out as expected, you'll end up happy; if not, you'll be angry or disappointed. Considering how often the second option happens, it's safe to say that having expectations sets you up for a lot of suffering.

Now, having fewer expectations doesn't mean not being optimistic about life or that you should stop goal setting; it just means you have the intention to be happy, or to be at peace, with "what is." Being more accepting of the reality that exists and the events that occur in your life actually helps you to look on the bright side. And it's an incredible way to be in relationship.

Lewis talks about his experience with expectations:

> After my second divorce, I considered remaining single for the remainder of my life. I thought maybe I would devote myself to spiritual pursuits without the distraction of another relationship. But in a conversation with a spiritual teacher I greatly respect, Sai Maa Lakshmi Devi, I learned that people can be in a relationship and continue their spiritual pursuits as long as they (1) have no expectations of their partner and (2) love their partner unconditionally. According to Sai Maa Lakshmi Devi, when one has expectations within a relationship, eventually those expectations will not be met. And that leads to resentment and anger which cause the relationship to spiral downward and become unhealthy.
>
> I have found that to be wise advice indeed. Now, I certainly recognize that it is not easy, or even doable, for most people, including me, to enter into a relationship without any expectations and to love their partner unconditionally all the time. But we can lean in that direction. These can be goals to move toward. And your expectations can

also be indicators of where you're "off" in your relationships. We ask people to try the following in our Madly in Love Forever Coaching. When problems arise, see if they can be attributed to unmet expectations and/or acting without unconditional love. If so, see if you can make a shift in the direction of accepting what is, and loving it unconditionally.

Here's an example of what I mean by expectations. They are mostly everyday kinds of things. Frequently, in the morning when I am getting ready to go to work, Diane will ask me if she can make me some eggs. I say "Yes, thank you." The next day when I get up, I do not expect that Diane will offer to make eggs for me. She may leave for work early, or choose to go for a walk instead of offering to make eggs for me. Since I have no expectation about her making eggs for me, when she doesn't, I am not disappointed; hence, I do not feel any anger towards her.

Note that the above situation is not to be confused with a situation in which I might have asked Diane the night before whether she would be willing to make breakfast for me and she agreed to. Diane and I believe it's important to keep the commitments that we make to each other.

Okay, there are eggs and then there's sex. The area of sexual relations is where I have been served the most by having fewer expectations. In my past, I had all sorts of expectations about how frequently sex should occur, how my partner should feel and react, and so on. Of course, my expectations were not always met, and when that happened I would get angry and feel sexually frustrated. Now I have far fewer expectations about sex, and I'm able to be spontaneous about when and how sex occurs. This makes the experience much more enjoyable and free of frustrations.

I learned a lot about living without expectations from reading and listening to Byron Katie, author of *Loving What Is* and a number of other books. Katie states that we suffer whenever we are not loving what is. So if I am expecting the world or my relationship or my partner to be a certain way and it doesn't happen, I must accept what is happening—unless I'd rather be sulky and unhappy. It's my choice. I can only change myself. Refusing to accept what is and trying to change it results in unhappiness. Changing myself such that I can accept "what is" brings happiness.

This isn't to say we can't work on ourselves and try to improve our lives and the world; that is a different concept. As individuals, we have control over our actions, and we can do tremendous good with them. But we can't control the actions of others, so it's best not to have expectations of what they'll do.

Being free of expectations is truly the ticket to enjoying emotional freedom. Give it a try and see for yourself.

Action Steps:

1. In your journal, write down the name of your partner, children, parents, siblings, friends and co-workers. List your expectations of these people.

2. Next to each expectation, jot down one or more effects it is producing in your life.

3. Make a list of the challenges in your life or your relationship. For each challenge, list one or more unmet expectations. Then, for each challenge, answer this question: How can I bring more unconditional love and acceptance to this situation? And: What would it take for me to be at peace with the reality of what is?

12. Control Freak No More!

"If you are the boss in your relationship—fire yourself!"

When we heard the leader of a relationship seminar say this, it gave us a good laugh while simultaneously appreciating the wisdom. If you insist on having everything your way in your relationship and having your partner do things the way you think they should be done, look out! This attitude puts any relationship at risk big time. It can turn a marriage into a dictatorship rather than a partnership, and historically, dictators are more likely to be shot than cherished and adored.

Worse still, if you're both trying to control each other, it can turn a relationship into a battle for the dictatorship. No wonder some homes feel like war zones!

What a relief it is to discover that making decisions together and giving your partner the space to do things his or her way can actually be a richer experience than always having to have everything your way. Not surprisingly, research clearly indicates that couples who make shared decisions in a smooth, comfortable way enjoy their relationship more. And please note, the shared decision may be that you agree to disagree and move on.

Diane reflects on how the control issue has affected her relationships:

> I am completely aware that I tried to control my partners in my past relationships. I did that because I was the "pleaser" type; you know, someone who's wondering all the time if she's keeping everyone happy. Now, think about it for a minute. If you are a pleaser, you may try to please your partner, which is good up to a point. But you also may start trying to control your partner so that he or she behaves in a way that pleases everyone ELSE you are trying to please.

This is a lose-lose situation. First, your partner's full expression of who they are is stifled. Second, you continue to be stuck being a pleaser. Better to be someone who stands secure in herself, not always trying to second-guess what others will like or not like. Oh my goodness, what a waste of energy! And yet so many of us, male or female, do just that.

This was a big problem in my first marriage. When Bob and I were by ourselves I easily accepted his ways. However, before we would join friends or family I might start "laying my trips" on him: "Don't talk about the fact that you are not materialistic," or "You better not bring up politics with my family."

Now, Bob was NOT a pleaser. Quite the opposite, if I may say. He was not at all concerned with impressing anyone or making anyone like him. He felt that he should always just be himself and let the chips fall where they may. So, not surprisingly, my efforts to control his behavior in order to meet my pleaser needs was not appreciated, and led to a lot of conflict between us.

Today, I'm very conscious of any tendencies to control Lewis, and I don't give them free rein as I did in the past. In my world of always looking for approval from others, I naturally sometimes imagine that people don't like certain things about Lewis. But now I am careful not to try to control his words and actions so that everyone will like everything about him. I've learned to mind my own business.

As a result, I am showing up much differently in my second marriage.

For example, Lewis loves to cheer loudly at his daughter's basketball games. Very loudly. And he loves to call out and encourage the young fans sitting in the bleachers to cheer more loudly and more often too. Sometimes I hear people say things like, "Hey, Lewis, chill out."

Sometimes people move away from us. At the same time, as I look around, I see lots of other people smiling up at Lewis.

The first time this happened, I remember hearing the old Diane say, "Uh oh," as I focused in on those who appeared to be annoyed at Lewis' loud cheering. I remember feeling tempted to tell him to be quiet. But as soon as I had that thought, I knew I was trying to control him in order to please the people who appeared to be annoyed. At that moment I flashed on one of our wedding vows: "I vow to honor your true expression and to celebrate that which is the highest and best in you without in any way limiting, **controlling**, hindering or restricting you." With that thought, I let go and enjoyed Lewis being Lewis.

Now, some people might think that I was giving in to Lewis and letting him have his way. In fact, I was rejoicing inside myself, feeling as free as a bird, because I had not given into my dysfunctional pleaser tendency. And what a treat it was to see Lewis cheering with all his heart, looking as though he was as free as a bird as well.

Can you see how Diane's choice not to control Lewis' behavior avoided a major confrontation and also led to greater emotional health and freedom for Diane? So often, when we take a step toward healthier behavior for ourselves, we also create more harmony in our relationship.

Lewis' thoughts on controlling and how to tell when you're doing it:

Controlling can be very subtle. Sometimes it is hard to distinguish between controlling and supporting. Here is an example:

A short while after we were married, I learned that Diane had not had a medical check-up in about four years. She shared with me that she was uncomfortable with doctors, hospitals and tests, and she felt like she was in great health, so it didn't seem necessary.

I felt concerned because I want Diane to maintain her excellent health for a long, long time. Now and again I would ask her if she ever thought about scheduling an appointment for a check-up. "Yes," she would say, "I know deep down that's the responsible thing to do and I appreciated your concern." Yet months went by and she still had not made an appointment.

If I were acting the way I used to, I would have used many different maneuvers, such as guilt-tripping and anger, to get Diane to go to the doctor. But now, being committed to not controlling Diane, I decided to be completely open with her about the doctor's appointment. I asked Diane if it was really important to her to go for her check-up. After ascertaining that it was, I asked her if she wanted some motivation to help her make the call to schedule the appointment. I reminded her that she uses "celebrations" as a reward for her coaching clients when they take a step forward.

"What would be a good celebration for you after you make the doctor's appointment?" I asked. Diane replied that she loved facials. We decided that right after Diane made her appointment, she would schedule an appointment for a facial. Guess what? She made both appointments!

Bottom line: Control hinges on whether or not I've asked for and have been given permission to give my input and make suggestions. I am being controlling if I step in when my partner hasn't asked for my help; on the other hand, I am being supportive if my partner agrees to accept suggestions and my support.

Control does not serve a relationship. If you get a sense that you are trying to control your partner, we recommend stopping immediately. If you want a healthy relationship, you have to let your partner be who he or she is.

In the action steps below, you'll get some ideas that will help you get over your habit of controlling.

Action steps:

1. List the ways that you think you may be controlling your part-
    ner. For example, do you yell, cry, dominate or give the silent
    treatment? Are you sometimes critical in a way that implies that
    no one else can do something as well as you?

2. The next time you feel the need to control, notice what you are
    feeling. Write about what you observed in your journal.

3. List some recurring situations that you tend to try to control.
    Choose one or more and write about how you could let go of
    controlling in that situation. Practice letting go the next time the
    situation occurs. Write down the results.

13. The Power of Appreciating Differences

*There is more hunger for love and appreciation
in this world than for bread.*

—Mother Teresa

We have heard it said that if you are judging your partner for the ways they are different from you, you are not loving them. If you are fighting those differences, we want to encourage you to make a 180-degree turn and begin to appreciate them. That's right—not just tolerate them, but actually see them in a positive light and appreciate them.

Why? For starters, any lack of appreciation is a lack of love and that's a blow to the relationship. As Marci Shimoff wrote in *Happy for No Reason*, "The best way to keep relationships happy, healthy and supportive can be summed up in one word: appreciation." Here's a reason from the scientists: Studies show that when a person feels acknowledged and appreciated, a neurochemical called dopamine, is released. The release of dopamine is directly linked to being happy. Who doesn't want a happy partner?! Another plus: it is said that being in a state of appreciation as often as possible puts you in a state of grace and abundance. Why? Because you are focusing on what you have, not on what you don't have.

These are just a few of the many ways to see the value of being appreciative. The bottom line is that we notice that happy couples appreciate each other. We see that these couples understand the value of appreciation and acknowledgement. And most agree it's simple to do, once you create the habit.

Yes, learning to appreciate is a habit. It's the habit of seeing the good in a person or situation.

Lewis shares a simple story that shows the effects of choosing appreciation.

It was a beautiful sunny summer afternoon. I had just finished mowing the grass with my ride-on mower. I got off the mower and sat on our picnic table, relaxing. I was content, sitting there, taking in the peace and quiet (now that the mower was off).

Diane came out of the house and commented on the beautiful weather. She then proceeded to unravel the garden hose, turn on the water and carefully spray the grass clippings off the sidewalk. Watching this, I began to chuckle inside. I would never have noticed the grass clippings on the sidewalk, and if I did, I certainly would not have thought to remove them. Years earlier, I would have judged Diane to be wasting her time and wasting water. I probably wouldn't have been able to refrain from mentioning this, thus putting a dent in the beautiful day for both of us.

Without the judgment, I was able to totally appreciate Diane. If I thought about it for just a second, I could see so many good qualities reflected in what she was doing. She was so good at keeping our home neat and beautiful. She noticed details that added up to creating a more orderly and pleasant environment. She was energetic and didn't procrastinate. And in doing all this, she was just being herself, doing what makes her happy.

As I noticed how different we were in the category of grass clippings, I also noticed how powerful using appreciation is. Instead of judgment and criticism, I felt a swelling of love for Diane. And the world felt like a perfect place.

From the picnic table, I could easily see our flower garden. In our garden we have yellow daisies, pink roses and purple lilacs. I cannot tell you which one I love the most, they are all so pretty. In fact, the uniqueness of each one adds to the beauty of the whole garden. In the same way, the uniqueness that Diane and I each bring to our marriage adds to its fullness.

Oh, and by the way, there's a purple lilac on my night table and a yellow daisy on Diane's.

 Some of you may be thinking that whether one waters the sidewalk or not is a pretty easy difference to accept. It is and it isn't. Our point here is, if you are arguing with your spouse, is it because you may not be accepting each other's differences? Are you constantly trying to get your partner to do things the way you do?

Diane's turn to share an experience:

> Lewis and I went to an all-inclusive resort in Mexico recently. Naturally the two of us wanted to orientate ourselves to this fabulous new environment that we were going to live in for a week. I immediately looked around to find a person, an employee, to speak with. I laughed to myself as I watched Lewis head for the maps and brochures. Notice I said laugh. In my prior marriage I might have been annoyed because in my mind it's faster and easier to talk to people. I might have judged my former husband for his actions. Now, I could laugh because I understand and accept the fact that people process and gather information in different ways. I was able to say to myself, there goes Lewis being Lewis, with a smile on my face.

> I thought to myself, it is imperative that couples get this! And so I share this simple example with you. In my mind I could hear all the potential fights and nasty comments we or any couple could have. I could have said to Lewis, "Come on, you're taking too long, just ask someone." Lewis could have said to me, "Diane, why do you think they created brochures and maps?"

> I mean, really, think about the things you fight about with your spouse. Is it over differences? If you find it hard to stop, at least stop judging your partner's learning or processing style, even if you can't appreciate or enjoy the difference immediately. Remember that

there's no one right way to do anything. Your way seems like the only right way to you because it's the best way for you, given your unique mental and physical processes. A very different way is probably right for someone else.

Now, of course, if you are dealing with a partner who is doing something that you actually think is wrong or illegal, you do NOT need to tolerate it at all, let alone appreciate it! Or if they are struggling with an addiction issue, they will probably require some kind of professional help, and you can be very strong about that. We are not suggesting that you try to accept any kind of behavior that violates your sense of what is right.

But in general, it's safe to say that a healthy, mature relationship allows for differences. Actually, we notice that the more comfortable we become within ourselves, the easier it is for us to appreciate and respect the differences in each other. Appreciation is a habit worth creating, and the key point is—it's a choice. You can always choose to appreciate. Remember that the next time you feel an urge to criticize or correct.

Action steps:

1. Appreciation is a technique for creating joy and tolerance and avoiding anger and conflict. Write in your journal about these questions: Are you judging your partner? Are you willing to take a step toward appreciating him or her instead? What would that look like?

2. Create a habit of appreciating your partner at least once a day. Carry a 3x5 index card or piece of paper in your pocket or wallet. Once a day write at least one sentence stating what you appreciate about your partner. Start with one comment, go to two comments and so on. Be realistic. It's okay to repeat the same one as you get started.

3. Ask your partner the following question: What makes you feel appreciated? Write his or her answers in your journal. Start showing your appreciation in these ways.

4. Make a list of five differences between you and your partner. Next to each difference describe how this difference makes your relationship richer, more interesting, more effective, or better still, more exciting.

5. Locate your wedding vows. Use the vows or create new vows that make strong references to honoring the essence of each other. Write these vows in your journal and read them frequently. Commit to honoring them.

PART III:

BUILDING A NEST WITH YOUR TRUE LOVE

Our turtle has been having *quite* a time. He's been getting to know some of the lady turtles in the neighborhood and has even gotten into a few relationships along the way. Quite a learning experience and a lot of fun too, for the most part.

But then, the other day…..there she was. Sitting on a log, the sun shining on her gorgeous shell, her dainty head lifted, intelligent eyes focused on a nearby dragonfly. She looked over at him…their eyes met…and that's the ballgame! True love had finally arrived. Oh, happy day! Time to build a nest and have a family.

Your story might be a little different. But when you find that special someone, it's a glorious day. And it's also the beginning of a whole new set of challenges to deal with, tools to acquire and lessons to learn. Fortunately, you've been growing in strengths and skills that will be there for you in the days ahead.

In Part III, we'll look from a number of angles at how to create a marriage or committed relationship that works. On the heart level, you'll learn how to nurture the relationship so it grows deeper and stronger with every year. On the physical level, you'll learn to create a sex life that zings. And on the very practical levels of finances, possessions and blending families, you'll get guidelines that will ensure your success.

Welcome to the beginning of being madly in love forever!

14. Take Time to Nurture Your Relationship

A dream you dream alone is only a dream.
A dream you dream together is reality.

–John Lennon

The vote is in and it's unanimous: Couples we talk to agree that when they give time and attention to nurturing their relationship, it is easier and more joyful to stay committed to each other.

Are you ready to make nurturing your relationship a priority? We assure you the results are worth the effort, whether you are in a new relationship or trying to rekindle a marriage. It doesn't matter what you did before or how much your relationship might have changed or even deteriorated over the years. It's never too late to create the relationship of your dreams.

We admire and give a lot of credit to couples who have managed to stay married for a long time. But the ones we bow down to are those who have not just stayed together, but actually stayed intimately connected—or become even more connected over time. They enjoy and support each other's growth year after year, despite all the challenges and changes that come with time.

What are the characteristics of those couples? Were they just lucky or did they consciously create the relationships they're enjoying? Luck may have a hand in it, but we think it's mainly the latter. You *can* create the long-lasting, deeply rewarding relationship you want.

How? We believe the main thing those couples have in common is that they are very aware of "the relationship" as an entity in itself, something to take care of. It won't thrive if it's neglected, but it will flourish if you create some quality time and space for it in your busy lives.

Here are some tips that have helped many couples build a thriving relationship:

- **Find time to be together on a daily basis.**

    Suppose you have a plant that needs to be repotted, and you don't have the time to do it. You would at least continue to water it, right? So it's still alive when you have time to repot it. In the same way, you need to take at least 5-10 minutes a day to nurture your relationship by connecting with each other in some meaningful way, whether by talking, cuddling or whatever!

    Sometimes that's all the relationship needs; ten minutes a day of "watering" and it's flourishing. Maybe these ten minutes happen in the morning before the busy day begins or late in the day when you get home from work. Maybe it's easiest when you're winding down in the evening or getting ready for bed together.

    Ideally, you can give each other your full attention in those moments and not be distracted by tasks. Have the intention to give your partner some love and support, and you will nourish your relationship and be rewarded with a happier and more loving partner.

- **Have regularly scheduled quality time together.**

    This point is a biggie. It's so important that you make a regular date, ideally once a week, to spend time quality time together— whether playful or serious.

    Now, we know all too well how busy everyone is, but if you want to be happy in your relationship, this is an ultimatum: Do whatever it takes to create a space in your busy lives for this weekly date. We have friends, married for over thirty years with four children, who, no matter what, get a babysitter on Saturday night and leave the house at 5:00 pm for a night out together.

The date could be dress up and go out for dinner, or grab a sandwich, park the car near a lake and connect. Sometimes the two of us make sacrifices because we feel that the relationship needs nurturing. This might mean we forego a party or other special event to spend some time alone together.

Find a date that's enjoyable, private, and rewarding for both of you. Sex can certainly be a part of it, but it shouldn't be only sex. Spend some time talking, whether in a light way or seriously, with a specific purpose or just exploring what's going on. You might want to spend some time being silent together too, if that feels more intimate.

- **Develop shared interests.**

  Lewis reports that when he joined a men's group many years ago he noticed that the men who were happiest in their relationships spent quality time with their partners in activities they both enjoyed. If you have no shared interests right now, can you imagine developing one or more? Can you both stretch to look into what your partner loves and see if there's an angle to it that sparks your interest? Maybe you'd love to take photos of your partner's stock car competitions. Maybe you could take an interest in wine if your partner is a great cook.

  This interest has to be genuine—and it isn't essential. Many happy long-term couples share no hobbies, and just have good times together and then enjoy their own pursuits separately. But it's good to explore the possibilities, just in case something works out, as this can really increase your enjoyment of time spent together.

- **Enjoy novel experiences together.**

  This is a good place to throw in some science, so here goes. When you first fall in love, the pleasure center of your brain goes into overdrive and certain brain chemicals are secreted in greater amounts. Some of these chemicals, including two called dopamine and norepinephrine, are associated with feelings of happiness, elation, greater focus and goal-directed behavior. So when you first fall in love, you literally are on a high!!

  As time passes and the love deepens, the intensity of infatuation wanes and these brain chemicals go back to normal levels. The balance you had in life before you fell in love returns, but it feels kind of deflating after the high you were on.

  So how can you stay madly in love when the chemical high wears off? Believe it or not, you can keep the pleasure centers of your brain active if you engage in novel and exciting activities together. When you experience feelings of happiness and joy together, you'll associate those positive feelings with each other and strengthen the bond between you.

  So go ahead and enjoy this science experiment: Make a commitment today to do something novel together. You could cook something new or go to a restaurant you've never tried before. How about taking a class together in some area you'd enjoy, such as art, yoga, fitness or computers? Is there a new project you could start in your home, such as planting a vegetable garden or doing some remodeling? Try volunteering for a community project or a special cause together. Creativity can spark infatuation, and so can having fun together.

- **Don't lose the thing your particular relationship needs to stay healthy.**

  Each person in the relationship needs certain things to stay alive and healthy—things like air, water, food, shelter, and affection.

Your relationship also needs certain things to keep it alive and healthy. What those things are depends on the two of you. By now hopefully you have a vision of your relationship and know your values, your lifestyle goals, your interests and your way of being. You can also consider this: what is essential to keeping your relationship strong?

In our case, we knew that sharing humor was important from the beginning. In fact, finding someone with a sense of humor was so important that "a good sense of humor" was at the top of both of our "ideal partner" lists!

And that is just what we found. When we first started dating, we laughed our heads off together. We remember saying to each other, "Let's make sure we always laugh together."

Well, life is busy, right? We notice that with busy comes a seriousness which can lead to a disconnected feeling. Do you know what we mean? So, if something funny doesn't just spontaneously happen between us, we *find* something funny to share. We search for hilarious You Tube videos, or even play ten to fifteen minutes of a funny movie from our own DVD collection.

Now, here's the important part: Rather than just laughing at the movie, we make sure we make eye contact, look at each other and enjoy the laughter and lightness on each other's faces. Honestly, being able to look at each other while laughing creates a special intimacy. It lightens us up and we associate that good feeling with each other. Just like sharing novel experiences, it's a way to turn individual enjoyment into nourishment for the relationship.

- **Take vacations together.**

Therapists and counselors have long known that vacations can mend and strengthen relationships. Have you ever noticed how happy couples seem after some kind of vacation or get-away together? Vacations rekindle the spark in the relationship. They create those new and novel experiences that stimulate the pleasure centers of our brains. Once again, the neat part is that you'll associate the happy feelings with each other.

If your next vacation together is months away, create a quickie vacation together this weekend of just one, two or three hours. You won't regret it.

- **Create your own rituals.**

    We read that it is sexier and more exciting to call routines you may have "rituals." Creating rituals can nurture your relationship.

    Diane shares a memory about rituals:

    Rituals make a lasting impression. My parents had a ritual when I was growing up. I remember that my mom would not walk away from the door after seeing my dad off to work till she couldn't see his face anymore. It made them laugh and feel connected. I remember to this day the sweetness of it all, watching my mom walk away from the door, smiling.

The two of us have a goofy one, and yet it leaves a smile on both of our faces. When we greet each other, we kiss three times. We share a laugh if one of us stops earlier than the three kisses.

We also practice a one-minute candle-lighting ritual that we learned while attending "The Couples 1 Seminar" with Rich and Char Tosi. This ritual is a minute well spent; it nurtures the relationship by creating a warm feeling between us.

Are you ready to nurture your relationship? Start enjoying more quality time together now and watch the love grow!

Action steps:

1. For the next month, each Monday, Tuesday, Wednesday and Thursday, have five minutes of completely uninterrupted time together: no cell phones, computers or children. Be present and do something to nurture the relationship. For example, rub each other's feet or backs, watch something funny or just lie together and hold hands; the possibilities are endless.

2. What attracted you to each other? Do something to enliven those qualities. We were attracted to each other's sense of humor, so we watch funny movies or You Tube videos and laugh, and that laughter nurtures our hearts.

3. Did you make your partner feel special when you first met? How did you do that? When was the last time you did something to make him or her feel special? If it wasn't recently, start planning something now. It might be something as simple as buying a card or flowers or a small present when it isn't a special occasion. Maybe it involves doing something you used to do together when you first met, such as going to your favorite restaurant or walking in a certain park.

4. Over the next two months, plan surprise romantic dates for each other.

    a. Put the dates on the calendar in advance as follows: "her surprise for him" and "his surprise for her."

    b. If you're inspired to, add a surprise during the day of the date.

    c. Be creative and stretch your boundaries a bit.

5. Attend a couple's workshop, go to a spiritual retreat together, or sign up for our Madly in Love Forever Coaching. These can be life changing.

15. Keep Sex Sweet and Sizzling

Have you ever noticed that sex is one of the first things to be affected when problems arise in your relationship? And that, once your sex life is thrown off kilter, it often becomes the central issue overriding all others?

We believe that a great relationship includes a mutually satisfying sex life—whatever that looks like for you. Obviously, there are no rules that apply across the board here. We encourage you to be real with each other and come up with the sexual relationship that works for you as a couple. Every couple is unique, and it's up to you to figure out the details of when, where, how, and how often is right for you (hopefully, 'why" is not an issue!).

That said, our suggestions in this chapter will probably work best for couples who are in a monogamous and committed relationship.

In our experience, the traditional stereotypes about men and women regarding sex are often untrue. For example, the stereotype of men just wanting sex and women just wanting to cuddle definitely doesn't hold true all the time. We see as many women as men who would like to improve the sex in their relationships.

One trend we've all seen growing is people having sex casually, sometimes without even any thought of getting to know the other person first. This isn't surprising, considering how our society flaunts sexuality everywhere—in movies, television shows, songs, magazines, live entertainment, and so on. But it's no wonder that some couples run into trouble because one partner wants to have that kind of freedom again.

When the two of us had the chance to start from scratch in a new relationship, we decided to act contrary to that trend. The other way just didn't work for us. Having rushed into two marriages very fast, Lewis was into taking it slower and being patient. Diane was feeling the same way. She had once heard at a seminar that people do more research and ask more questions when they're buying new cars and homes than when they're thinking about being with a potential partner! Think about it; don't you want to know more about a person you're getting that intimate with?

As a result of this mindset, we dated casually for about ten months without having a physical relationship. Yes, ten months! Call us troglodytes! It wasn't until we began to feel more serious about each other and decided to date each other exclusively that we wanted a change. At that point, we were aware of the inevitability of moving into a physical relationship.

You can imagine how much we wanted this experience to be comfortable and rewarding for ourselves and each other. Here we were, both over 50, and of course—with five children between us—far from virgins, but both wanting a more satisfying and richer experience. And that's what we got. Being conscious and moving slowly allowed us to delve into and relish each stage of our romance.

We believe we learned about each other's sexual needs and wants more thoroughly this way than we would have with the "Wham, bam" approach. With empathy, any awkwardness, emotional baggage, performance anxiety and more was addressed. Again, this is what worked for us, and you may be different. But we feel that, with this approach, we created an environment for a more open, passionate and ultimately satisfying sexual relationship for ourselves over the long term.

The following sections cover some of the issues that could arise over the course of your physical relationship. In every case, our first suggestion is to try being courageous and frank with your partner. Discuss these issues openly and often, and experience the benefits that come from your talks. Remember to use what you learned in Chapters 9 and 10 in these talks. The best solutions are the ones you work out together.

TEAM WORK: It Takes Two

In previous relationships Lewis experienced the following situation:

> She would say yes, she wanted to make love. Why, then, was I feeling like she was resisting? She seemed to think making love was something I was doing to her, not something we were doing together.

When two people love each other, it's natural for both to want to express their love physically, so genuine, heart-felt lovemaking is always a cooperative endeavor. It's not a solo flight! Both of you must be willing to be open, active and present during lovemaking. Both of you must be willing to state what you want and what doesn't work for you.

WHEN: Whenever!

Some folks are morning people and others are night owls. This applies to sex too. Because sex usually happens in bed, people tend to automatically think that the best time for sex is at night when we get into bed. But for some people, that might be the worst possible time.

For many, getting a good night's sleep is very important and when they get into bed, all they are interested in is sleep. This doesn't mean they don't want to make love; they just want to do it at another time—maybe in the morning or during the lunch hour or before dinner or before bedtime. You have to talk about what works for you and come to some agreements, and maybe even compromises.

Another issue is the epidemic of over-scheduled lives, such that you're too busy for sex during the day and too exhausted when you conk out at night. If your schedules are hectic, you may need to plan regular "dates" with your partner just for lovemaking. If you value your relationship, you have to include your sex life somewhere in your priorities, work it into your schedule and use some discipline to make sure it happens.

Children can be an obstacle to lovemaking, but you can overcome it. Hire sitters and trade with friends and family in a routine of "you mind theirs, they mind yours." It is so easy *not* to do this! But if you don't, you will wake up one day and find that your sex life is dead.

It is hard work but you MUST set up some arrangement so that you can have a healthy, ongoing sex life. Not to do this is to invite loss of connection and drifting apart, not to mention infidelity. And you *can* do it; it may not seem humanly possible, but it is! Again, discussing and deciding when to make love is an important first step.

What about spontaneity? Go for it!! What about keeping a slow fire going throughout the day or the week via emails, phone calls, notes? By all means!! Any way in which you can pay attention to your partner's sexual energy is highly recommended. Stoke that fire, and you will enjoy the heat! Neglect it and your home and your hearts will get chilly.

FREQUENCY: The Art of Compromise

We laughed and saw the profundity in this scene from a Woody Allen movie:

> The man in the relationship is complaining to his therapist that his wife never wants to make love to him, so they only have sex three times per week. The scene changes to the wife complaining to her therapist that all her husband can think about is sex, and so they make love all the time—three times a week!

Frequency of lovemaking is a classic problem in relationships. It's a tough one—people simply have different sexual appetites. Not only that, our sexual appetite is subject to change. It's affected by many things: age, season, illness, pressures at work or home, and issues within the relationship, to name just a few.

If you have this conflict—and in our experience, most couples do—here's a compromise that many have found helpful: Agree to have a "quickie" to satisfy your partner when he or she is interested and you are not. The key here is for the one who's not so into it to truly enjoy his or her partner, as opposed to feeling annoyed or resentful. It's just a few minutes; can you give your partner that small bit of time and effort for the sake of more sweetness between you?

As we see it, there is no magic number for how often to make love. The important thing is the happiness of both partners, and the willingness to make compromises on both sides. So this is another area where you have to do some talking. Use your best communication skills to speak honestly about your sexual appetites, and practice putting your "love in action" as you try to meet each others needs and serve each other as best you can, within reason and comfort.

This area can take some persistence, and some trial and error, and you may have to find within yourself a lot of tenderness, humor and forgiveness. But the reward is great if you stick with it until you find a rhythm that works for you as a couple.

WHERE: Guess!

This one is easy. ANYWHERE! We made a game once of making love in every room of our house, inside and out. You get the gist. A change of scenery adds spice to your sexual routine. This opens up the opportunity to explore being more creative, or use more of your existing creative energy.

Once we drove about a quarter of a mile from our country home and went parking. Our SUV had plenty of room and a great sound system. We felt like teens again, adding even more fun to our relationship. Both of us being originally from New York, we saw this as another advantage to country living! And the thought of being caught at our age by some young Iowa State Trooper added an extra thrill of danger!

93

HOW: State Your Preference

Unless you skipped to this chapter first, you know that we are big on taking responsibility for our own life. Sex is no different. You cannot assume your partner knows what you want. You must communicate your needs and wants to your partner. Now, we know this is not so easy for most people. People who have no problem asking their partner to take out the garbage or to make spinach pie suddenly become shy when it comes to asking to be kissed or caressed in a certain way. A lot of us were raised not to talk about such things. But you've got to get comfortable with asking for, or in some way indicating, what you want. Good sex is not for mind-readers!

Some couples find this is easier if they make a game of it. Take a look at the chart below, showing four possible actions for two partners. Start with any category and spend an entire lovemaking session with actions inspired by it. Or, alternately, move through two or more boxes in a single lovemaking session. Another time see how many different ways you can fulfill each task. When you're both experimenting and trying new things, shyness falls away pretty fast. And it's okay to collapse in giggles, too!

He asks her to pleasure him in a particular way	She asks him to pleasure her in a particular way
He does something to her that brings pleasure to him	She does something to him that brings pleasure to her

If you can include actions from all four quadrants at times in your lovemaking, both partners will be happy.

When to Cuddle, When to Couple

There are times in your relationship when one of you will need a little nurturing. Perhaps your partner had a fight with a friend or lost a key account at work. When your partner's spirits are low, you may be the best one, even the only one, to comfort him or her. This is a time when your skills as a listener or massager come in handy. Just being present for your partner will go a long way toward cheering him or her up, and he or she will be very appreciative. But be aware that this may not be the time for sex, unless your partner specifically asks for it. Your partner may need all his or her energy just to bounce back from the setback. And, it's possible that if you initiate sex at this time, your partner may think your nurturing was a ploy for sex and lose that wonderful feeling of unconditional love and support. Again, it's all in the communicating!

Want that lovemaking glow again? OK, then…time to take action!

Action steps:

1. Set a time to discuss your physical relationship honestly and openly. Discuss what you are doing that you like, what you don't care for and what you are open to trying. Thank your partner for being open and sharing with you.

2. Experiment with making love at different times of the day. Talk about which ones you like best. Continue to vary your routine whenever possible, as you like.

3. Make love in a place where you never have before. We're sure there's at least one! If you find you enjoy this adventure, continue to find more places for lovemaking.

4. Have "quickies" as needed to stay connected and open to each other.

5. And…slow it down sometimes. On a regular basis, consciously spend extra time on the early stages of lovemaking. Enjoy kissing and caressing, and linger in that tender stage. It is said "a man is like a stick of dynamite ready to go off at any moment and a woman is like a fire waiting to be lit and tended into a roaring bonfire."

16. Seeing Yourself in Others, Revisited

There is no place to hide from the mirror of intimate relationship.
Our partner reflects both our inner beauty, but also the ways
in which we are unconscious.

—Robert and Judith Gass

You may remember that in Chapter 5 we introduced the concept of the mirror, which basically states that we can learn a lot about ourselves by observing our reactions to those around us and taking responsibility for our feelings. As we said, the mirror analogy works in two ways:

- In the "If you spot it, you've got it" situation, you're judging a quality in another person only to discover, upon reflection, that it's bothering you because it's a quality you have too, and wish you didn't.
- With "The world is as you are," you are reacting to a situation negatively, only to realize that your reaction is based upon your present state of mind (which includes your unhealed childhood wounds) more than anything outside yourself. You recognize that your interpretation of outside events is being colored by feelings you're carrying inside.

In both cases, the mirror can dissolve our negative feelings by showing us where they're really coming from. Of course, we mirror each other in these ways all the time in our intimate relationships. Becoming aware of it can strengthen our relationship and also increase our ability to take responsibility for our own stuff.

Here's an example from Lewis of how the "If you spot it, you've got it" mirror can serve you in your relationship.

> Some years ago, Diane was working long hours to complete her Life Coach training. She was busy taking classes, writing papers, coach-

ing and being coached. One day I felt really neglected. I thought to myself, "She likes her work more than she likes spending time with me. She's a workaholic!" I felt sad and left out and a bit resentful.

Now, it was time for me to look into the mirror. I thought, what is going on here? I know Diane loves me, so why am I feeling slighted? Does this show up somewhere else in my life? After a minute or two, I had an "ah-ha." At some times of the year, my job requires me to work long hours, frequently going in at 7:00 a.m. and working until 7:00 p.m. I was seeing my own undesirable "workaholic" behavior in Diane! Once I realized that when I work long hours, I am not rejecting Diane, I was able to stop judging Diane and to see that Diane's long work days were not a rejection of me.

If you feel a lot of negativity toward someone, this may be a mirror screaming at you: you spotted it, you've got it! As unlikely as it may seem at first, we've found that we can always locate in ourselves some form of what we're judging in others, if we're genuinely open to looking for it.

Diane shares a story that illustrates how the mirror can show us that "The world is as you are":

Lewis and I were having lunch at home one day, when I start telling him about all the things I had done that morning. Lewis' reaction appeared neutral; he looked like he was listening but he didn't say anything. I began to wonder, "Does Lewis approve of what I did this morning?" In that instant, I slipped into my wounded state and became angry and afraid. I was unconsciously remembering how my father found my mistakes, or "holidays," as I described them in Chapter 5. I felt I was being unreasonably judged and criticized.

In the past, I would have reacted defensively and apologetically. My fear would have caused me to withhold information and possibly even tell some little white lies. Now, with the knowledge of the mirror, I realized that my angry and fearful feelings had nothing to do with Lewis. He was just sitting there listening to me, and I was creating all this upset in my own mind, based on experiences from my past.

When I remembered to stick to "Just the facts, ma'am" and not make assumptions about what Lewis was thinking, I relaxed and felt comfortable again. Instead of being unhappy, I went back to enjoying our time together.

Can you find times in your life when you felt angry or defensive towards your partner? Can you see how it may have been triggered by a similar quality in yourself or a childhood wound?

The concept of "The world is as you are" isn't always about wounds from the past. It also applies to our everyday state of consciousness in that however we are feeling at a particular moment affects what we see in our environment. On a "good hair day" when you are feeling terrific about yourself, it is easy to feel grateful and appreciative towards your partner.

But what about the times when you are having a "bad hair day"? Maybe you come home from a tough day at work and find your partner has made a snack in the kitchen and left things out all over the counter. Okay, it's not the end of the world. But because you're grouchy and tired, you might start to feel bitterly resentful that you "have to do everything around the house." Before long you may find that you're saying to yourself, "I wish I weren't in this relationship." If there's negativity inside us, it will color everything we see around us, wherever we go.

"The world is as we are." Just remembering those words can break the spell. What you're seeing isn't the absolute truth, it's the truth distorted by a certain filter your mind is holding up right now. The environment is reflecting back your own negativity. What a relief to realize, "Oh, I'm just in a bad space right now! I can't believe anything I think about what I see around me. It's just my own unhappiness being reflected back at me."

We know how easy it is to move into blaming each other, but here, and in our Madly in Love Forever Coaching, we urge you to try using this mirror concept instead. It provides such insight—and in real time, in your face! It's usually very hard to see ourselves as others do. Well, this is one way you can do that. It's another very profound way of taking responsibility for your own life.

Lewis shares a way in which this concept ties in with the concept of gratitude, discussed in Chapter 7.

> When I use the mirror and see that a situation is all about me, not Diane, I stop blaming her. Instead, I welcome this opportunity to look at myself. Then I feel gratitude for Diane and our relationship; they are allowing me to see and face something within myself that, when confronted and healed, will make me more whole as a person. Then, not only will I be better off, I will also be better able to love Diane for who she is.

One final point: It is counterproductive to try to push away the feelings we do not like, such as anger, jealousy and insecurity. If we try to push these feelings away, they will remain and probably get even stronger. So, instead, we must welcome these feelings and acknowledge them. Once a feeling is acknowledged, we can examine its source or origin, and opportunities for releasing it. Frequently, these negative feelings served legitimate self-protection roles in an earlier time of our lives. However, now that we are older, those same feelings are no longer necessary and can be limiting.

In the action steps below, you'll find exercises that will help you practice using the mirror and responding to what you see there. We believe that this concept alone can turn a relationship around 180 degrees. However much conflict you may be experiencing, it can melt away when you realize that the true conflict is going on within yourself.

Action Steps:

1. In your journal write down a quality in your partner that pushes your buttons. Can you find any aspect of that quality in yourself? If yes, how do you now feel about your partner having it too? Write about your discoveries.

2. Make a list of childhood memories, asking yourself, "What experiences did I have that still affect me today?" For each experience, write about how it affects you and also your relationship with your partner.

3. Can you relate to the "bad hair day/good hair day" discussion above? If so, think about what you can do during down times to remember not to project your negativity onto your partner. Write down your thoughts and share them with your partner.

17. Putting Your Finances on the Table

When you find your true love, naturally you want to be together and create a new life together. Whether you marry or choose to live together, you have many practical issues to address in the transition from single to shared living. There are now two financial situations to deal with, two sets of possessions to merge, and perhaps two sets of children coming together under one roof. Financial issues are a significant factor in divorces.

How to handle such seemingly complicated and delicate issues lovingly, intelligently, and harmoniously before, during and after the transition into a shared space?

We suggest that you plan ahead. Talk about issues such as money, children, pets, possessions, holidays, and relatives, before you walk down the aisle or call the moving van. Take the time while "love is in the air" to communicate everything you can about these fundamental topics. Put your interviewing skills to work! Interviewing and planning will force you to examine some of the specifics of how your relationship will work in the future. What an opportunity to establish a foundation of honesty and mutual respect in your communication!

In this chapter, we will focus on your finances. Merging households and children will be tackled in the next two chapters.

We can't advise you on the specifics of how to handle your finances, but we can tell you we are big believers in sorting it all out before you make a move. Whether you are planning to cohabit or marry, now is the time to be honest and upfront about all your expectations, assumptions, desires, intentions, and boundaries around money.

This may surprise you, but we are also big believers in creating and signing a prenuptial agreement. And even if you aren't getting married, we believe it's a great exercise to look at a sample pre-nup together or both read a book about them, as it gives you a great opportunity to discuss all the issues that arise when you look closely at your finances.

Diane talks about how she became a believer in having a pre-nuptial:

> I clearly remember the day Lewis suggested the concept of pre-nuptial agreements. For a few seconds I thought, "What?!" Then I looked into Lewis' eyes, took a deep breath and realized the logic behind prenuptial agreements. I hated to think about this marriage not working, but I realized that if for some godforsaken reason it did not, I would be spared the enormous conflict over finances that usually comes with divorce. Having to deal with that, on top of the emotional pain of my divorce, had been devastating for me.
>
> So, one beautiful spring day we took books about prenuptials to the park with us and, with love in the air, proceeded to plan our future with everything out on the table. We ended up, after several such meetings, with a prenuptial agreement that only deepened our understanding of each other and our mutual trust.
>
> Time and time again in the years we've been married, I've appreciated that we chose to do this as a couple. Having discussed it all in detail back then, we know exactly where we stand financially and have very few issues around money as a result.

We urge you, no, we implore you, to do the same and have some kind of prenuptial agreement in place before you marry. We know that sounds dramatic, and it is, because we believe waiting until after marriage to discuss important financial issues sets a marriage up for failure, or at least a lot of conflict. Many couples find themselves saying or hearing things like this: "You didn't spend money like that when we were dating," or "You didn't tell me about that debt while we were engaged," or "Why don't you buy me nice presents anymore?"

Why do we change when we get married? We're only human and as human beings we want to be loved. So it's tempting to act a certain way while courting each other because we feel it will increase our chances of being loved and having a relationship. In Chapter 8 on dating we expressed our opinion on this. We feel it is unfair to act one way while dating and appear differently after marriage. Yes, it's tempting, but it isn't necessary. Better to grow in self-knowledge, self-love, and clarity and develop a strong sense of who you are. Then it becomes less important to change for anyone. Imagine two people loving themselves and coming together to create a relationship based on giving their love to each other. That's what we really want.

Can you see the pain that can be spared if you sort out your issues before you enter the journey of marriage? If so, you're probably wondering, "What questions should I ask my partner?" "What if I forget something important?" "You can't predict everything." Or you may be thinking, "We are so in love, we don't need to do a prenuptial agreement"

These are valid questions and concerns. Please use the books and action steps below as guides to the prenuptial process. They suggest all the pertinent questions you can ask your potential partner. We were happy to see that the experts in prenuptial agreements suggest revisiting your agreements every few years. At the end of this chapter are more action steps for you to take.

There's an old saying, "Avert the danger that has not yet come." That's how we see a prenuptial; as a way to "prevent the birth of an enemy." We hope we've inspired you to check it out for yourself!

Action steps:

1. If you are getting married, broach the subject of a prenuptial agreement with your partner. Assuming one or both of you are not familiar with the content of prenuptials agreements, commit to reading one book about them and having a discussion afterwards. We suggest *Prenups for Lovers* by Arlene G. Dubin and *How to Write Your Own Premarital Agreement* by Edward A. Haman.

2. As a prelude to a discussion about prenuptial agreements, write in your journal what is important to you around money issues, such as earning money, saving money, accumulating assets and leaving an inheritance for children.

3. If you are moving in together without getting married, write in your journal on the points in #2, and share what you've written with each other. Then write a financial plan together that sets the guidelines for the ways in which you will and will not share finances going forward.

18. Making Two Households One

When you remarry or live together, you and your partner (if he or she has been married before or had his or her own place) will probably have to combine two households into one. Obviously, you are going to have duplicates of many items. Therefore, before you start combining your lives and possessions, consider that this might be a good time to de-clutter and simplify your lives and bring fresh creative energy to your new life. Bringing two lives together is complicated enough without carrying a lot of unnecessary physical baggage along for the ride!

Having less clutter can also help make times of transition easier to handle emotionally. Diane relates her experience in this area:

When I went through my divorce, things were chaotic and unpredictable, to say the least. To stay sane and grounded, I kept my home environment as orderly and clean as I could. In times of extreme pain, confusion and frustration, I would look up and see my clean and orderly home and be reminded that things were not that bad. I'd feel, "I can handle this," or I'd tell myself, "Not everything is falling apart." In the midst of pandemonium I could feel some peace. My grown children to this day thank me for keeping things stable and organized for them at a heartbreaking time.

Realizing the power in organization and stability, Diane became an organizational coach, which helped supplement her income from teaching elementary school. Diane has assisted clients in organizing their homes, cars and offices. Clients sense her passion for simplicity and appreciate that she adds a sense of fun and support, knowing how hard getting organized and letting go can be for some people.

Diane feels the best part is getting to see color and light come back into people's faces, as they said goodbye to broken, incomplete and old items. She had one client who actually got up and danced with joy at the new space and energy created by de-cluttering. Others have said, "Gosh, I feel like I lost weight or something!" and "I'm not so bogged down any more."

Diane's experience in this area helped us enormously when it came time to combine our households. We knew that, in addition to the general weeding out of items we no longer wanted or needed, there were also two processes unique to prenuptial de-cluttering. The first was deciding which of the duplicate items to keep and which to sell or give away. The second involved each of us deciding which items were so connected to our previous marriage that we didn't want to carry them forward into our new life. Diane suggests passing these items on to your children. If your children are young, store the items in a special box that can be given to them later.

As you're sorting through your belongings, there are two questions to ask as you decide whether to keep an item or not:

- Do I need it?
- Do I use it?

If you answer "no" to both, be ruthless! Give it the old heave-ho.

It works best to use the "four category" system. Set up a box or bag for each category:

- Throw Away
- Charity
- Not Yet
- Seasonal

The Not Yet box, full of things you know you don't really use or need but can't bear to part with yet, goes to a friend's house for about six months. Anything you don't ask to have back within that time gets given away by your friend.

Even with thorough de-cluttering, we realized that our combined possessions were too numerous to be displayed or used all at once. Diane solved this problem with a seasonal rotation system that makes use of all the precious items each of us had—just not all at the same time. All the items in your seasonal category can be displayed in rotation, according to the current season or holiday, using your walls, shelves, desk tops and cabinets. We rotate not only spring, summer, fall and winter items, but also our Jewish and Catholic holiday items. We find it makes our home homier when attention is given to the special times in our lives.

One more tip on seasonal rotation. Have fun with it! Step into your inner child for a while! Enjoy how fresh and new your decorative items feel when you're not looking at them constantly.

The exciting discovery about de-cluttering is that with less stuff and better organization you can have more lightness and energy, and begin to create more time for the important things in your life, like, oh my gosh, your loved one!

Action steps:

1. Commit to sharing the job of organizing and de-cluttering. It helps a lot if both partners are involved, though you'll probably be doing some tasks on your own and some together.

2. Coordinate your timing. Mark the day or days in your planners that you will devote to de-cluttering and organizing.

3. Start small. We did one closet at a time, then our garages and so on.

4. Get help if the task is daunting. Consider hiring "clutter busters" or ask your children or friends to help. Make sure they are ruthless!!

5. See the job through to the end. There can be a tendency to store bags and boxes that were meant to be thrown away or taken to Goodwill. Clear them out and see how clean and fresh your living space feels.

19. Creating a Blended Family Your Kids Will Love

Warning! Thorough Preparation Is Essential
To Survive This Extremely Worthwhile Endeavor!

What do we mean by thorough preparation? We mean reading and doing the exercises in the previous chapters. Whether you are about to blend families or are already in a blended situation, we feel this will strengthen you, put you in touch with who you really are, prepare you to take responsibility for what you are creating and inspire you to make changes, if need be. In our opinion, it takes two very strong, committed, flexible, and open-hearted people to blend two families successfully. And the first step is to take a deep breath, be ready to let go of old stories and perhaps be willing to change the way you've been doing things.

Now that we've scared the daylights out of you, let us give you some words of encouragement!

We believe in the possibility of a happy, functional blended family. We believe that being part of a loving family is a blessing. If couples planning to marry take the time to prepare for the challenges of blending two families, this new marriage and new family arrangement can be a chance to model love's resilience. Children can witness not only their parent experiencing love again, but also behaving in a more loving manner with another adult.

We believe that witnessing loving behavior has a healing effect and restores faith in children that marriage can work. It's an opportunity to show children that sometimes life is one way and then it turns out to be another way. When they see the parent pick up the pieces after a painful experience and create a new loving experience, they know that love can always spring up anew.

It is our hope that the work we do on ourselves, on our relationship and on the new family arrangement will inspire our children to choose their partners wisely, enjoy happy marriages and stay married! How beautiful to think of this love spreading to our children's children and so on. Imagine if all of us could stop the painful cycle of divorce. If you believe in the institution of marriage as we do, then it's worth taking the time to understand what you are getting into when you blend two families and take steps to do it right.

In today's world, blended families are more common than ever. In America there are 15 million step children under the age of 18. As a result, there are a lot more opportunities for couples to learn about how to make them work. Unfortunately, only about 25% of couples seek out help, which is pretty sad considering that second marriages have a high divorce rate, in large part because of the challenge of blending families.

We've heard it said that the process of blending families is somewhat like building a house. It takes time, planning, endless adjustments as you go, cooperation from everyone involved and adequate resources, mixed with plenty of patience, tolerance and understanding. Each situation will have its own set of circumstances and its own challenges.

As soon as we started thinking about getting married, we addressed the concept of blending our families. We thought about the issues involved and dealt with them in very honest discussions. Now we hear comments from the two children who still live with us that sound like this:

> "I feel like I have a bigger family. Things feel more fun," commented Nofiya.

> "Sometimes I miss living in town, but I drive now and having a sister live with me is cool," said Lucas.

Diane's son, Lucas, doesn't see a lot of his biological father as he lives far away. Lucas tell us he appreciates Lewis' male energy in his life. He went as far as to say he hates using the word "step" when he talks about Lewis and Nofiya. He calls Nofiya his other sister.

How was this happy situation created? Before we planned our wedding, we did as much "homework" as we could on this topic. One of our regular dates during our engagement period was to research information related to the issue of blended families. Combining fun, coffee and treats while doing our research at a popular bookstore in the mall closest to our town, was a wise choice for us.

During that time, we ended up reading a lot of books, manuals and magazines, and we took the advice we received to heart. And, most important, we practiced the concepts we learned. Over time, we found certain guidelines that we believe are most important for successful family blending and committed to following them. Now, it's true that we had an easier situation than many: as we've mentioned, three of our children were already living independently when we got married, and we only had two high-school students at home, a girl and a boy. So, we ran these points by families that had successfully blended younger children, and they agreed that our guidelines were appropriate.

They *all* wished they had prepared more. Here are a few common pieces of advice that were the golden threads through all our conversations with them:

- **Prepare** by reading books or by talking to couples who seem happy in their blended family and see what they did to make it work.

- **Be alert** to where you are emotionally when you enter a relationship. If one or both of you is needy, remember, you are dragging children into this scene. Will it be difficult for them? Are you both ready to be as grounded, mature and giving as you need to be with children? The advice is: Don't rush to merge your families if you don't both feel strong and centered.

- **Blended families are challenging** because they have all the issues traditional families have—chores, teenagers, college, money, sharing of parental attention and resources, personality conflicts, and so on—and then they have many additional issues. Somehow the blended family has to move through all these issues with even more sensitivity. There are many more people involved, such as former spouses, more grandparents and step-siblings, so the parents must be their wisest and most mature selves to keep it all working smoothly.

- **Give it time.** Putting pressure on stepchildren to accept and love the new family can breed resentment. So be patient.

Lewis and Diane agree wholeheartedly with the above and add a few of their own tips because they have worked for them and hope they help you.

- **Communicate with your children.** Discuss everything. Don't bottle up emotions or hold grudges. We had a biweekly family meeting to discuss any issues that were up. Now that our children are both seniors in high school, we rarely meet because of their full schedules, but all is going well because we set the stage for open honest communication with them early on.

- **Spend time with your own child.** Once a week we each have a special lunch date with our child. This gives us a chance to check in with them and maintain our pre-marriage relationship with them. This is a perfect opportunity to see whether anything is up for our child in this new blended family environment. We are happy to report that both children look forward to this special lunch.

- **Change as little as possible for the children.** Only change towns, schools, etc. if absolutely necessary. We have been lucky; we live in the same town so our children stayed in their schools and did not leave the other parent.

- **Sometimes one set of rules does not fit all.** We initially thought we were going to have the exact same rules for our two high school students. Lucas and Nofiya like each other, go to different schools and live different lifestyles. But it caused friction between them when we tried to have them on the exact same schedule with the exact same rules. So, when necessary, we adjusted the rules to suit each child.

> For example: Lucas always did his homework with friends who lived nearby and he was allowed to be out until 9:00 pm to do so. Nofiya did her homework alone at home for the most part. Diane started to tell Lucas he had to do homework alone at home too, believing that was the fair thing to do. Lucas resented the change and brought this to our attention. We then realized not every rule was going to be the same. We acknowledged the different learning styles that worked for each child and respected the choices we each made around our children before we married. We allowed Lucas to do his homework as he always had. Nofiya never questioned the rule anyway as she continues to do homework in her style.
>
> Our point here is to be aware, flexible and open to the possibility that you may have to tweak your rules to suit each child. Remember that this will help the children adjust more happily to the new blended situation.
>
> It's important to note here that both children are subject to the same house rules, such as having regular chores, doing their own wash and keeping the common areas of our home clean and orderly.

- **Don't interfere with your partner's parenting**. An important question each partner must ask him/herself is this: Can I live with the way my partner parents? If you answer no, you may not be able to live with your partner. If you answer yes, then make a promise to yourself and your partner to do so. And as you go along in your marriage, remember that promise. Do not suddenly start criticizing or judging situations that come up with your partner and his or her parenting choices.

Now, if your partner asks for help in parenting, go for it. One of you may be more comfortable handling a certain aspect of parenting, such as discipline. Don't be afraid to ask your partner for comments about how you are handling something, and be open to hearing what he or she has to say. As in any parenting situation, the interests of the children should be paramount, not your pride in how you have handled situations prior to your remarriage.

- **Avoid criticizing your partner's child.** Here's the truth—whether it's reasonable or not, parents can get very defensive when it comes to their children. We notice this in ourselves and with other couples we have talked with or coached. Feelings of resentment can come up if your partner has even a little too much to say about your child's behavior, especially if the comments are critical.

So, to sum up, learn everything you can about dealing with blended families, plan ahead, make sure you can live with the way your potential partner disciplines his or her children and make a commitment to your partner not to interfere in his or her parenting choices. Don't enter the marriage thinking that you will change anything or that eventually it will all be going your way. If you do, you are in for problems.

To all couples we say, let's model loving and harmonious behavior whenever possible! Children thrive in the presence of a stable, loving relationship between the adults in the household. We nurture their souls when they feel harmony between the numerous adults involved in raising them. This is reason enough to have read our book and to join our Madly in Love Forever Coaching.

Action Steps:

1. Clean up your relationship with your ex-spouse as best as you can. This will make interactions surrounding your children smoother.

2. Clarify with your new partner what role you see him or her playing in the rearing of the children you are bringing into the marriage.

3. Discuss with your children what changes will be taking place in their lives. Find out how they feel about this. Ask them to share their thoughts and feelings with you whenever new situations arise in the new family situation.

4. Read, read and read as much as you can on blending families. There is no such thing as being over-prepared in this arena.

Now Go Out and Love Madly!

Reading this book won't change anything. Change will only occur in your life if you take action. Our final and most important message to you is this:

**If you want a better relationship, do something different now!
Choose action!**

It's amazing what happens when you put your thoughts into action. As a matter of fact, we wrote this book and developed our Madly in Love Forever Coaching hoping it would inspire you to want to change some things about yourself and how you show up in your relationship. We hope you are inspired to use our action steps now and in the months and years to come. Getting into action without delay is a habit worth creating.

If you are in Hell, start moving toward Heaven now. If you are close to Heaven and don't want to slip back, take action now.

If you are madly in love and want that love to last forever, use this book as a checklist to make sure all your bases are covered and practice one or more of our action steps every day.

If we have rekindled your awareness of concepts and practices you already knew, great.

If you have learned new concepts and practices, fantastic! Now use them every day.

It doesn't matter where your relationship is today. What does matter is your commitment to change the habits you know you need to change, to transform your life for the better and to move ahead with all speed toward enjoying the relationship of your dreams.

If only one partner is ready to change and grow at this time, go for it, and see what happens in your marriage. It's a start. And whatever the outcome, we assure you, you will never regret having begun this journey.

Join the many couples who hold the vision of a better world where husbands and wives are happy and where children can grow up in homes filled with love and security.

We thank you for spending time with us, and, with all our hearts, we wish you good luck on your journey to being madly in love forever.

Enjoy!

Notes

Notes

Notes

Notes

Notes

Notes

6405461R0

Made in the USA
Charleston, SC
20 October 2010